Linda's *summer* Kitchen

Linda's *summer* Kitchen

LINDA McCARTNEY

FOOD CONSULTANT
Rosamond Richardson

PHOTOGRAPHY
Debbie Patterson

To my family and all veggies,
present and future

A Little, Brown Book

This edition produced for The Book People Ltd,
Hall Wood Avenue, Haydock, St Helens WA11 9UL
by Little, Brown and Company
Reprinted in 1997

The recipes were originally published in Great Britain in 1995
by Little, Brown and Company in *Linda's Kitchen*
Introduction copyright © 1995 and 1997 by MPL Communications Ltd
Text and Photographs copyright © 1995 and 1997 by
Little, Brown and Company (Inc.)

ISBN 0-316-639788
A CIP catalogue for this book is available from the British Library

Food styling by Jane Suthering
Design by Janet James
Typeset by Peter Coombs
Sun illustration by Nadine Wickenden
Printed and bound in Italy by Lego Spa

Little, Brown and Company (UK)
Brettenham House, Lancaster Place, London WC2E 7EN

The author would like to thank Paul, Heather, Mary, Stella, James, Louise, Robby
and team, Viv and team, Carol Judy and team, Geoff, Pat, Sherrie, Marie,
Sue, Shelagh, Louise, Laura, Monique, Ann, Mike, Ian, Tim and team, John, Sharon,
Maxine and everyone who helped and shared a veggie recipe.

Contents

INTRODUCTION

When my husband asked me why I was writing another cookbook, it made me realize how time had flown – and how far vegetarian cuisine had progressed in the intervening years. When I wrote my first cookbook, it was to show my family and friends how easy it was to become a vegetarian. But now our eating habits have changed, most of us are trying to cut down on fatty foods, and I felt the time had come to bring things up to date and to increase the range of easily prepared recipes that are available to today's cook.

Even if you find cooking daunting, I hope to bring out the creative cook in you. It may be that you've always thought of vegetarian meals as tiresome to prepare and bland in taste – in which case there's a surprise in store for you. Vegetarian cooking is easy, it's tasty, and it's good for your body too. Recent research has shown that a vegetarian diet can dramatically lessen the risk of – amongst other things – heart disease, angina, cancer, diabetes and high blood pressure.

Some people believe that they are vegetarian if they just cut out red meat, but a vegetarian eats no meat, and no fish either. If you go veggie, it means no animal dies for your plate. I've met a lot of people who say, "I'm almost veggie, but I still eat fish." To me that's like being "almost pregnant" – either you are or you aren't. I know that for some people cutting out fish is the most difficult obstacle on the road to vegetarianism. But fish have feelings too, and anyone who has ever seen a fish hooked out of the water, jerking and gasping for breath, should realize that. The "bountiful sea" does *not* exist for us to plunder at will, and perhaps if we started thinking in terms of sea*life* instead of sea*food* our appetite for fish might be lost.

Of course tradition is responsible for much of today's meaty diet. For most of us in the West, meat and two veg is a standard meal and, for many people, Sundays are not complete without a roast meat dinner. But the world has changed since those traditions developed. Many more people share this planet and, as the population grows, it is simply not going to be possible to feed everyone on a meat-based diet. There just isn't enough grazing land for all the livestock required.

For me, that's a good enough reason in itself for becoming a vegetarian – because if we fed the starving people of the world the grain we use to fatten farm animals there really could be enough to go round. If everyone in the West reduced their meat consumption by just ten per cent, it would free up enough grazing land to grow food for up to 40 million people. So, being a vegetarian is not only better for you, it's better for everyone.

There are other lives that will be saved if you go veggie – the lives of the millions of animals that are slaughtered every year.

Butchered in such horrific ways that if slaughterhouses had glass walls, we'd all be vegetarian. So, be a life-saver and a world-saver, and start a whole new way of life.

There are meals for all to enjoy here – from vegan meals to meals for the truck driver who reckons he'd miss his meat (...but he won't), to kids' meals, low-calorie meals, meals for entertaining and family meals. While you're cooking, don't be afraid to adapt these recipes to suit yourself. I've tried to make taste the main ingredient in all of them; so get into the kitchen, rattle those pots and pans, have fun, and save lives while you're doing it – yours, the animals' and the planet's.

Linda McCartney

SUMMER MENU PLANNER

A TEENAGERS' PARTY FOR 15

Enchilladas (x2) 26

Mexican corn bread (x2) 23

Nachos (x2) 22

Easy pizza 65

Bean tacos 22

Burritos 20

Carrot salad 78

American soured cream dip 90 with tortilla chips

Chocolate delight (x2) 95

Carrot cake 102

A LUNCH FOR 6

Summery tomato soup with dill 13

Summer lasagne 48

Carrot salad 78

Mixed leaf salad with soy and lemon dressing 83

Frozen vanilla mousse (x2) 100

Vegan fruit cake 101

A BARBECUE FOR 12

Dill cucumber dip (x2) 91 with crudités

American soured cream dip 90

Marinated vegetarian sausages and burgers (x2) 68

Crusty garlic potatoes (x2) 71

Vegetable kebabs (x2) 69

Char-grilled mushrooms with rosemary and garlic (x2) 68

Courgettes with herbs (x2) 70

Mexican corn bread (x2) 23

Barbecue sauce 87

Salsa 88

Roasted red pepper sauce 87

Tarragon and mustard sauce 89

Selection of salads

Peaches and butterscotch 72

Praline bananas (x2) 72

A Buffet for 24

Guacamole 90
with crudités

Aubergine purée (x2) 18

Vegetable
spring rolls (x4) 60

Summer lasagne
(x2) 48

Vegetable
quiche (x2) 61

Spinach pancakes with
mushrooms (x3) 42

Lemon
green beans (x3) 28

Simple saffron
rice (x2) 50

Fennel salad 78

Spicy raw
mushroom salad 76

Shredded courgette
salad 77

Avocado, mozzarella
and tomato salad 77

Cheesecake made
with strawberries 94

Fruit sorbet (x2) 99

Pecan pie 94

A Dinner Party
for 8

Asparagus soup (x2) 12

Stuffed peppers (x2) 32

Quick meatless
stroganoff (x2) 39
with rice

Courgettes with
sweetcorn (x2) 27

Watercress salad with
garlic croutons (x3) 74

Raspberry mousse (x2) 92

Floating islands 100

A Romantic
Dinner for 2

(HALVE ALL RECIPES)

Aubergine purée 18

Vegetable
mille-feuilles 63

Rosti 57

Special rocket salad
with spinach
and Parmesan 76

Tiramisù 99

An Anniversary
Celebration for 12

Aubergine purée (x2) 18

Provençal pepper
salad (x2) 80

Savoury vegetable
strudel (x2) 58

Summer lasagne
(x2) 48

Watercress salad with
garlic croutons (x2) 74

Redcurrant
cheesecake (x2) 94

A Mediterranean
Menu for 4

Artichoke dip 89

Garden soup
with pesto 10

Best vegetable
paella 36

Provençal pepper
salad 80

Fruit sorbet 99

SOUPS

ONE OF THE JOYS OF COOKING WITHOUT MEAT IS MAKING SOUPS, USING THE ABUNDANT HARVEST OF FRESH INGREDIENTS WITH THEIR VARIED COLOURS, FLAVOURS AND TEXTURES. SPICES ENHANCE THE FLAVOURS, AND FRESH HERBS ADD QUALITIES ALL THEIR OWN. SOUPS ARE HIGHLY NUTRITIOUS AS WELL, FULL OF VEGETABLE PROTEIN, AND RICH IN VITAMINS AND MINERALS.

GARDEN SOUP WITH PESTO ᵥ

FOR 4–6

3 tbs olive oil

1 clove garlic, crushed

1 medium leek, sliced thinly

2 large carrots, diced

1 small turnip, diced

2 small potatoes, peeled and diced

2 pints (1.2 litres) vegetable stock

6oz (175g) frozen peas, thawed

1 small crisp lettuce, shredded

1 tbs chopped fresh tarragon

¼ pint (150ml) simple pesto sauce (see page 90)

sea salt and freshly ground black pepper

grated cheese (optional)

Utilizing the early summer vegetables from the garden makes this a light, refreshing soup.
It is so pretty to look at, too, with the contrasting fresh greens and the orange of young carrot.
Vegans can omit the garnish of grated cheese.

METHOD: Heat the olive oil in a large saucepan and sauté the garlic, leek, carrots, turnip and potatoes for 5–6 minutes or until beginning to soften. Pour in the stock and bring to the boil, then leave to simmer for 15–20 minutes or until the vegetables are tender.

Add the peas and lettuce and simmer for a further 5 minutes. Stir in the tarragon and pesto and season to taste. Serve with a bowl of freshly grated cheese to hand around.

ASPARAGUS SOUP

FOR 4

2 tbs vegetable oil

1 onion, finely chopped

1 medium potato, peeled and diced

4 stalks celery, finely chopped

1 pint (600ml) vegetable stock

8oz (250g) fresh asparagus, tough ends of stalks removed, chopped, or equivalent canned asparagus, drained and chopped

sea salt and freshly ground black pepper

milk to thin the soup if necessary

The delicate flavour of asparagus comes through well in this attractive pale green soup.
If fresh asparagus is not in season, substitute canned – the result will be just as delicious.

METHOD: In a large saucepan, heat the oil and cook the onion until soft and translucent. Add the potato and celery and cook for a further 2 minutes, stirring. Pour in half of the stock and bring to the boil, then cover and simmer for 10–15 minutes or until the potatoes are tender.

Add the asparagus and the remaining stock. Cover again and cook for 10 minutes or until all the vegetables are tender.

Ladle half of the vegetables into a blender or food processor and purée. Return to the pan and stir to mix with the remainder of the soup and vegetables. Season to taste and heat through. If the soup is too thick, thin with a little milk.

COURGETTE AND WATERCRESS SOUP ⓥ

FOR 4–6

3 tbs olive oil

2 Spanish onions, sliced finely

2 pints (1.2 litres) vegetable stock

2lb (1kg) courgettes, trimmed and chopped roughly

2 bunches watercress, stalks trimmed

sea salt and freshly ground black pepper

fresh lemon juice

This lovely green soup has a distinctive, subtle flavour and is a treat served with hot garlic bread, or with croutons for a contrasting crunch. If you want a creamy, non-vegan version, add some crème fraîche or thick plain yogurt just before serving.

METHOD: Heat the oil in a heavy saucepan and stir in the sliced onions. Cover and cook them over a low heat for 10–15 minutes or until tender and sweet. Add the stock and bring to the boil, then add the courgettes. Simmer, uncovered, for 15 minutes or until they are very tender. Remove from the heat.

Add the watercress to the pan, stir well and cover. Leave to stand for 5 minutes.

Strain through a sieve set in a bowl. Set the liquid aside and purée the solids in a blender or food processor, or press them through a sieve, until perfectly smooth. Return them to the pan and stir in the liquid. Reheat the soup. Season to taste and add a little lemon juice to sharpen the flavour. Serve at once.

SUMMERY TOMATO SOUP WITH DILL v

FOR 4–6

3 tbs olive oil

2 large onions, sliced finely

2 large cloves garlic, crushed

bunch of fresh dill, chopped

3 pints (1.75 litres) vegetable stock

1 x 1½ lb (750 g) can tomatoes, or the same weight fresh tomatoes, skinned (see page 36) and chopped

1 tsp ground allspice (optional)

pinch of sugar (optional)

sea salt and freshly ground black pepper

finely grated rind of ½ orange

4 fl oz (125 ml) soured cream (optional)

sprigs of fresh dill to garnish

A fresh, summery soup, ideal served chilled for lunch on a warm day. Use home-grown tomatoes for the best flavour.

METHOD: Heat the oil in a saucepan and stir in the onions. Cover and cook gently for 10 minutes, stirring occasionally, until completely soft and sweet.

Add the garlic and cook, covered, for a further 5 minutes. Stir in half of the dill and cook, uncovered, for 3–4 minutes.

Pour in the vegetable stock and add the canned tomatoes with their juice or the chopped fresh tomatoes, the optional allspice and sugar. Season with salt and pepper. Bring to the boil and leave to simmer gently for 35–40 minutes.

Add the orange rind. Remove from the heat and allow to cool slightly. Purée the soup, in batches, in a blender or food processor until it is quite smooth. Add the remaining dill. Return it to the pan, unless serving cold, and heat through very gently for 5 minutes. Correct the seasoning and serve, with a dollop of soured cream on each serving, if you like, and garnished with a sprig of dill.

GAZPACHO ANDALUZ ❤

FOR 6

2 slices granary bread, crusts removed

2 tbs olive oil

3 tbs fresh lemon juice

3 cloves garlic, crushed

1 x 1½ lb (750g) can tomatoes, or the same weight fresh tomatoes, skinned (see page 36) and chopped

2 canned pimientos, drained and chopped, or 1 large fresh red pepper, chopped

6 spring onions, chopped

½ cucumber, roughly chopped

¾ pint (450ml) tomato juice

sea salt and freshly ground black pepper

2 tbs mayonnaise (optional)

For the garnish a selection from:

black olives

finely diced cucumber

chopped green pepper (or red or yellow)

cubes of toasted or fried bread

finely diced raw onion

finely chopped tomatoes

finely chopped parsley

A wonderful chilled soup with refreshing tastes, full of natural vitamins. Serve in small bowls with the garnishes to hand around.

METHOD: Soak the bread in the olive oil and lemon juice, with the garlic, while you prepare the vegetables.

Put everything, apart from the seasoning and mayonnaise, into the blender and run until smooth. Season to taste and stir in the mayonnaise, if using. Chill thoroughly before serving. Hand around the garnishes so that everyone adds their favourite.

CROUTONS ❤

Add croutons to soups for extra texture or for a more filling meal. Using garlic makes the croutons even tastier.

Remove crusts from 4 slices of bread and cut into tiny cubes. Heat vegetable oil gently in a frying pan and fry the bread cubes over a medium heat, shaking to turn them until they begin to turn golden and become crisp. Add 1 clove of crushed garlic towards the end of cooking, keeping the heat down to prevent the garlic from burning. Stir the garlic croutons thoroughly. When evenly browned (be careful not to overcook them) remove the croutons from the pan with a slotted spoon and drain on kitchen paper.

Keep warm in a very low oven until ready to use.

SWEETCORN CHOWDER

FOR 4

2 potatoes, peeled and cut into ½ inch (1.25cm) cubes

¾ pint (450ml) water

1 onion, chopped

2 tbs olive oil

1½ lb (700g) fresh sweetcorn kernels (see below) or 2 x 14oz (400g) cans sweetcorn

¾ pint (450ml) milk

4fl oz (125ml) single cream

sea salt and freshly ground black pepper

paprika to taste

pinch of dried thyme

1 bay leaf

freshly chopped parsley and chives, to taste

A great American classic, this creamy golden
soup is easy to make.

METHOD: Parboil the potato in the water, salted, for 10 minutes. Meanwhile, cook the onion in the oil over a low heat, covered, for 5–8 minutes or until translucent. Add the onion to the potatoes with the remaining ingredients and bring back to the boil.

Leave to simmer for 20–30 minutes or until the sweetcorn is tender and the soup is slightly thickened, stirring occasionally. Discard the bay leaf before serving.

STRIPPING CORN KERNELS OFF THE COB

Remove the outer leaves or husks and all silk from the corn. Holding the corn cob upright with the flat end firmly on a board, run a sharp knife down the length, between the kernels and the cob, to strip the kernels away.

VEGETABLE STOCK v

MAKES – as much as you like!

vegetable trimmings, such as onion, carrot, leek, cabbage, tomato, broccoli, cauliflower, Jerusalem artichoke, potato peelings

cold water to cover

sea salt

black peppercorns

2 bay leaves

fresh or dried herbs

This is the basis of many soups. It is worth
getting into the habit of making stock regularly, so that
you always have some when you need it.

METHOD: Put the vegetable trimmings into a large saucepan and cover with cold water. Add a little sea salt, a sprinkling of black peppercorns and the bay leaves. Add a small bunch of fresh herbs, such as sage, parsley, thyme, chives and/or tarragon, or 1 tablespoon of dried mixed herbs.

Bring to the boil and simmer, covered, for 45 minutes. Then leave until cold. Strain, and store in the refrigerator for up to 5 days.

LIGHT MEALS AND SIDE DISHES

HERE YOU'LL FIND AN EXCITING RANGE OF SNACKS, STARTERS AND SIDE DISHES THAT YOU CAN MAKE QUICKLY AND EASILY. THE SELECTION OF MEXICAN RECIPES DEMONSTRATES THE VERSATILITY OF THE TORTILLA, WHICH IS USED IN TACOS, ENCHILADAS, BURRITOS AND NACHOS. THESE MAKE SATISFYING QUICK MEALS, HIGHLY NUTRITIOUS BECAUSE THEY OFTEN CONTAIN REFRIED BEANS OR VEGETARIAN MINCE.

AUBERGINE PURÉE v

FOR 4

2 large aubergines

juice of 2-3 lemons

2½ tbs tahini (sesame paste)

3 tbs sesame seeds

1 large clove garlic, crushed

sea salt

4 tbs chopped parsley

1 tbs olive oil

This Middle Eastern dip is also known as 'poor man's caviar', although it is just as luxurious as the real thing. Serve with toasted triangles of pitta bread or carrot sticks.

METHOD: Pierce the aubergines several times with a sharp knife. Bake at 190°C/375°F/gas 5 for 30–40 minutes or until soft. Set aside to cool for about 30 minutes.

Peel the aubergines and discard the skin. Put the flesh in a bowl and immediately add the lemon juice. Mash well, or blend in the food processor. Add the tahini, sesame seeds and garlic and mix in thoroughly. Season with salt.

Spoon into a serving dish, cover and chill. Before serving, sprinkle with parsley and drizzle olive oil over the top.

CHEESE AND NUT PÂTÉ

FOR 4

1 slice wholemeal bread, crusts removed

3 fl oz (75 ml) skimmed milk or soya milk

5 oz (150 g) walnut pieces or pecans

3 oz (75 g) Cheshire cheese, grated

1 large clove garlic, crushed

2 tbs olive oil

freshly ground black pepper

sprigs of parsley to garnish

Crunchy and garlicky, this pâté makes a great start to a meal, or a light lunch in its own right with a tossed salad, such as the special rocket salad on page 76.

METHOD: Soak the bread in the milk. Blend the nuts roughly in a food processor – not too smooth because you want the pâté to have texture. With a fork, work the nuts, cheese, garlic and oil into the soaked bread. Season with lots of pepper. Press into a mould or terrine, and chill.

To serve, turn out and garnish with sprigs of parsley. Eat with thin toast or baby tomatoes, celery and carrot sticks and a selection of other crudités in season.

MEXICAN SNACK FOODS

This selection of Mexican recipes demonstrates the
versatility of the tortilla. All make wonderful and satisfying
quick meals which are also highly nutritious.

THE VERSATILE TORTILLA

Tortillas are the Mexican version of pancakes,
made of wheat flour or corn (maize). They are the basis
of tacos, burritos, enchiladas, nachos and quesadillas.

METHOD: Taco shells are corn tortillas folded in half and
fried crisp. You can buy taco shells, or you can make your
own by frying tortillas, using a ladle to make a hollow in the
centre (see page 22). Fill with one of the fillings on pages
21–22, or invent your own. For authentic Mexican flavour
add canned mild chillies to your mixture – they will not
blow your head off as fresh chillies are apt to do!

BURRITOS AND CHIMICHANGAS

A burrito is a warm wheat-flour tortilla filled with
vegetables (often including beans or refried beans),
made into a parcel and topped with salad.

METHOD: Put the filling of cooked vegetables, beans,
grated cheese and shredded salad into the centre of the
warm tortilla, fold the bottom quarter over, then the sides,
then the top, to make an envelope. Serve immediately.

For a Chimichanga simply fry the filled burrito in shallow
oil until golden brown. Serve with a Mexican salsa (for
home-made version, see page 88), guacamole (see page 90)
or soured cream.

QUESADILLAS

A quesadilla is a turnover, made with a wheat-flour tortilla and fried lightly in oil. Here refried beans and cheese provide the filling.

FOR 1 (Makes 2)

2 small wheat-flour tortillas

2 tbs canned refried beans, thinned out with a little water

2 oz (50g) cheese, sliced thinly

2 tbs bottled taco sauce or home-made salsa (see page 88)

sliced fresh chilli (optional)

vegetable oil for frying

METHOD: Spread the tortillas with the refried bean mixture and place the sliced cheese on top. Dot the taco sauce or salsa on the cheese and add a slice or two of fresh chilli if you like things spicy-hot!

Fold the tortillas into half-moon shapes and fry in a very little oil in a hot pan until browned on both sides and heated through. Eat immediately.

TACOS WITH TOMATOES AND VEGETARIAN MINCE ᵛ

This is a really tasty snack meal, with its appetizing mixture of textures, flavours and colours. Vegans can make these omitting the cheese topping.

MAKES 8

12 oz (350g) vegetarian mince

2 tbs olive oil

2 oz (50g) almonds, chopped

2 small onions, sliced finely

2 cloves garlic, sliced finely

3 tomatoes, skinned (see page 36) and chopped

a little tomato juice to bind

sea salt and freshly ground black pepper

1-2 tsp cayenne pepper

8 taco shells, warmed

3 oz (75g) grated cheese

shredded lettuce

METHOD: Brown the vegetarian mince in 1 tbs oil for 3–4 minutes, then add the almonds and cook until they are browned too. In a separate pan, soften the onions and garlic in the rest of the oil. Stir in the tomatoes and juice and cook until well amalgamated. Season to taste with salt, pepper and cayenne. Add the mince and almond mixture and stir well.

Fill the warm taco shells. Top with grated cheese and shredded lettuce. Serve with salsa (see page 88).

BEAN TACOS WITH RED PEPPERS ▾

MAKES 8

1 tbs olive oil

1 onion, sliced

1 red pepper, deseeded and chopped

1 x 14oz (400g) can pinto or kidney beans, drained (or equivalent cooked dried beans, see page 106)

4 tbs chilli sauce

1 lettuce, shredded

8 taco shells, warmed

3oz (75g) Cheddar cheese, grated

soured cream

Memorable tastes which linger on the palate
and make a snack meal with a difference.
As with the other tacos, vegans can eat these if
they omit the cheese and soured cream.

METHOD: Heat the oil and soften the onion and red pepper for 5 minutes. Add the beans and cook uncovered for 10 minutes. Mash, and then mix in the chilli sauce.

Put shredded lettuce into the warm taco shells, spoon the warm bean mixture over the top, and top with cheese and soured cream.

TORTILLA SHELLS

Deep fry a corn tortilla in very hot oil, pushing the centre down with a ladle. Cook until golden – half a minute or so. Remove the ladle and allow the tortilla to finish cooking until golden. Drain on kitchen paper and dry. Fill the central hollow with any of the fillings on pages 21–22, top with grated cheese and finish with shredded salad.

NACHOS

FOR 6–8

5oz (150g) tortilla chips

8oz (250g) mild Cheddar cheese, grated

6 tbs bottled hot taco sauce (optional)

These are just brilliant! If your family is hungry
and looking for a very fast snack, make these nibbles
instead of opening a packet of potato crisps.

METHOD: Spread the tortilla chips one layer deep in shallow baking dishes. Sprinkle with the cheese and dot the optional sauce on top. Bake at 200°C/400°F/gas 6 for 5 minutes. Serve immediately and eat at once!

SPICY REFRIED BEAN TACOS v

MAKES 4

8 oz (250 g) canned refried beans

2 tbs bottled taco sauce or salsa (see page 88)

4 medium tomatoes, skinned (see page 36) and chopped

4 spring onions, sliced finely

1-2 tsp hot chilli relish

sea salt

4 taco shells, warmed

grated cheese (optional)

shredded lettuce

sliced avocado

soured cream (optional)

Rich and filling, a snack meal for the hungry!
Crisp taco shells are filled with a spicy tomato and bean mixture, shredded lettuce and grated cheese,
and topped with avocado slices and soured cream.
(Vegans can omit the cheese and soured cream.)

METHOD: Heat the refried beans with the taco sauce or salsa. Add the chopped tomatoes and mash thoroughly. Add the spring onions and cook gently for 4–5 minutes, stirring frequently. Season to taste with chilli relish and a little salt.

Half-fill the warm taco shells with the mixture and top with grated cheese and shredded lettuce (you can put the lettuce at the bottom of the shell if you prefer). Garnish with a slice or two of avocado and a dollop of soured cream.

MEXICAN CORN BREAD

FOR 4–6

1 free-range egg

2 tbs olive oil

½ oz (15 g) fresh green chillies, chopped very finely

6 oz (175 g) canned sweetcorn, drained

4 fl oz (125 ml) crème fraîche

4 oz (125 g) yellow cornmeal (polenta)

1 tsp sea salt

1 tsp baking powder

8 oz (250 g) Cheddar cheese, grated

This is nothing less than beautiful – spicy,
cheesy and very more-ish! Serve it warm from the oven,
or reheat slices in a microwave for 30 seconds.

METHOD: Beat the egg with the oil until blended. Add the chillies. Stir in the sweetcorn, crème fraîche, cornmeal, salt, baking powder and all but 2 oz (50 g) of the cheese. Pour into an 8–9 inch (20–22.5 cm) shallow cake tin. Sprinkle the remaining cheese over the top.

Bake at 180°C/350°F/gas 4 for 40 minutes. Cool slightly in the tin, then turn out and serve warm.

OVERLEAF: Mexican Feast with Soured Cream Enchiladas (see page 26), Corn Bread, Tortillas piled with mixed vegetables and Guacamole (see page 90)

ENCHILADAS

Enchiladas are the Mexican equivalent to our stuffed pancake –
wheat-flour tortillas are rolled up around
a tasty filling and then baked, often topped with a spicy sauce.

SOURED CREAM ENCHILADAS

MAKES 6

6 *wheat-flour tortillas*

3 *tbs salsa (see page 88) or light tomato sauce (see page 86)*

4oz *(125g) chopped onion*

4oz *(125g) cheese, grated finely*

½ pint *(300ml) soured cream*

olives to garnish

These are rich and succulent, ideal for a casual
summer meal with friends, served with a tossed salad.
To make the meal more substantial, add Mexican
rice 'n' beans (see page 50).

METHOD: Brush the surface of each tortilla with some salsa or tomato sauce. Mix the chopped onion with the grated cheese and half of the soured cream. Put this filling into the centre of the tortillas and roll them up. Place seam-side down in a baking dish. Cover with the rest of the soured cream, and bake at 190°C/375°F/gas 5 for 20 minutes or until golden.

Garnish with olives and hand more salsa or tomato sauce around for those who want it.

TRADITIONAL ENCHILADAS

MAKES 4

8oz *(250g) vegetarian mince*

2 *tbs vegetable oil*

½ *small onion, chopped finely*

4oz *(125g) cheese, grated*

4fl oz *(125ml) crème fraîche or soured cream*

¼-½ *tsp chilli powder*

4 *wheat-flour tortillas*

This tasty dish is highly nutritious. The creamy
filling is rolled up inside tortillas which are
then baked. Serve with a salad of crisp green leaves
and orange segments.

METHOD: Sauté the vegetarian mince in the oil. Mix with the onion, cheese, crème fraîche and chilli powder and use to fill the tortillas. Roll them up and bake seam-side down at 180°C/350°F/gas 4 for 10–12 minutes or until hot through and crisp on top.

CHEESE ENCHILADAS

MAKES 6

2 tbs sweetcorn relish

4 oz (125 g) Cheddar cheese, grated

2 oz (50 g) shredded iceberg lettuce

4 canned tomatoes, drained and chopped

3 spring onions, chopped

6 wheat-flour tortillas

6 tbs soured cream (optional)

This is a wonderfully simple snack meal, or it can be a light supper served with rice and a tossed salad such as the watercress salad with garlic croutons on page 74 or the carrot salad on page 78.

METHOD: Mix together the relish, cheese, lettuce, tomatoes and spring onions and roll up inside the tortillas. Bake seam-side down at 190°C/375°F/gas 5 for 20 minutes or until the tops of the tortillas are crisp and lightly browned. Top with soured cream, if using.

COURGETTES WITH SWEETCORN ◊

FOR 3-4

2 tbs olive oil

1 lb (500 g) courgettes, cubed

12 oz (350 g) canned sweetcorn, drained

1 small onion, chopped

1 large clove garlic, crushed

small handful of fresh tarragon, chopped, or 1 tbs dried tarragon

sea salt and freshly ground black pepper

This simple recipe is easily prepared, and its colours are delightful – yellow and green glow off the plate.

METHOD: Heat the oil in a large frying pan and add all the ingredients. Cook gently, stirring, for 5 minutes or until they begin to soften. Then cover with a lid and cook over a very low heat for a further 5 minutes. Check the seasoning and serve hot with saffron rice or plain noodles.

CHILLIES

Chillies come from a large botanical family with many varieties. You see them in the shops in all sizes and colours – red, green, cream and even purple. The plump green jalapeño chilli is popular and used in many Mexican dishes. Chillies vary in strength so err on the side of caution: start with a little and then add to taste.

Dried chillies are a useful standby and can be very hot. Canned chillies, however, tend to be milder and are a truly delicious way of spicing. Beware of chillies in vinegar – they blow your head off.

ASPARAGUS WITH GARLIC

FOR 4

2-3 cloves garlic, crushed

4 tbs olive oil

2lb (1 kg) asparagus

4-6 tbs finely grated Parmesan cheese

2 tsp fresh lemon juice

When asparagus is in season,
make the most of it and try this unusual way of serving it,
with garlic-flavoured oil,
lemon juice and freshly grated Parmesan.

METHOD: Mix crushed garlic to taste with the oil and set aside. Stand the asparagus spears upright in a tall pan of boiling water (the tips should not be submerged), cover and cook for 8–10 minutes or until tender. Lift the asparagus carefully into a colander to drain.

Arrange the asparagus on warm plates and spoon the garlic oil over the tips. Sprinkle with Parmesan and lemon juice, and serve immediately, with warm crusty bread to mop up the juices.

LEMON GREEN BEANS ᵥ

FOR 3–4

8oz (250g) fine green beans

2oz (50g) margarine

3 tbs fresh lemon juice

sea salt and freshly ground black pepper

3 tbs chopped parsley

With grilled tomatoes and pitta
bread, this fresh-tasting vegetable dish will
make a lovely light meal.

METHOD: Steam the beans for 3–4 minutes or until slightly softened. Melt the margarine in a pan and stir in the beans. Cover and cook over moderately low heat for about 5 minutes or until tender.

Add the lemon juice and season to taste. Cook for a further 3 minutes, then sprinkle on the parsley. Mix well, and put into a serving dish.

OPPOSITE: Asparagus with Garlic (top); Lemon Green Beans (bottom)

JUICES

Vegetable and fruit juices are not only delicious, they are renowned for their health-giving qualities. They are full of flavour as well as being packed with minerals and vitamins. These nutrients are absorbed very quickly into the body, and have a fast revitalizing effect. Juices are best drunk as fresh as possible, although you can keep them for several hours in an airtight jar in the fridge. For best results use a good electric juicer.

FRUIT JUICES ▾

These are deliciously refreshing at any time of year, and always best when the fruit is in full season. Try squeezed juices: orange, grapefruit, lemon and tangerine; or juices extracted in an electric juicer: apple, apricot, blackberry, blueberry, blackcurrant, grape, kiwi, mango, melon, pineapple, pear, peach, papaya, plum, raspberry, strawberry. You can mash banana and add it to the above.

Some aromatic mixtures are:

banana and peach	mango and orange
banana and berries	peach and apricot
banana and apple	pineapple and peach
pear and apple	grape and apple

Or you can mix fruit and vegetable juices. The variety is endless, and you will enjoy trying out all the different combinations possible as the seasons turn. Some suggested combinations are:

carrot and apple	cucumber and peach
apple and celery	cucumber and apple
carrot and orange	celery and pineapple

VEGETABLE JUICES ▾

Carrot, tomato and cucumber juices are very pleasant drunk straight. If you prefer you can mix them with a small amount of strong-tasting juices such as spinach, lettuce, cabbage, celery, beetroot, parsley or watercress, which are too strong to drink on their own in any quantity.

You can make excellent 'juice cocktails'. Serve them on ice garnished with fresh herbs.

Here are some delicious combinations:

carrot, beetroot and cucumber
carrot and cucumber
cabbage, celery and tomato
tomato and alfalfa sprouts
carrot, celery, tomato, pepper, spinach and beetroot with a touch of parsley and watercress

MAIN COURSES

WHEN IT COMES TO THE MAIN COURSE, SOME PEOPLE STILL FEEL THAT A VEGETARIAN DISH IS NOT AS SUBSTANTIAL AS A MEAT ONE. MEAT SUBSTITUTES HAVE BEEN ADDED TO SOME OF THE RECIPES IN THIS CHAPTER, BUT THEY CAN EASILY BE OMITTED AS THESE DISHES ARE DELICIOUS IN THEIR OWN RIGHT.

STUFFED PEPPERS v

This dish is inspired by the cookery of the Middle East, where stuffed vegetables of all kinds play an important part. You can make the stuffing with vegetarian mince or without, adding another 2 oz (50 g) rice in its place if you prefer.

MAKES 6

3 peppers

1 large onion, chopped finely

2 tbs olive oil

1 clove garlic, crushed (optional)

8 oz (250 g) tomatoes, skinned (see page 36) and chopped

3 sun-dried tomatoes in oil, chopped (optional)

3 tbs chopped parsley

1 tsp each ground cumin and allspice or to taste (optional)

1/2 tsp chilli powder (optional)

4 oz (125 g) vegetarian mince

3 oz (75 g) long-grain rice, cooked (see page 52)

2 oz (50 g) pine nuts

METHOD: Halve each pepper and scoop out the seeds.

Soften the onion in the oil for 7–8 minutes over a low heat, covered with a lid. If using the garlic, add for the last 2–3 minutes of cooking. When soft, add the tomatoes, the optional sun-dried tomatoes and the parsley and stir well. Then add the optional spices and cook gently for a minute longer. Stir in the rest of the ingredients.

Pack the mixture into the pepper halves. Place in a large greased baking dish or roasting tin. Pour in hot water to cover the bottom of the dish, cover with foil and bake at 190°C/375°F/gas 5 for 30 minutes. Remove the foil and bake for a further 15 minutes.

STIR-FRY OF SPRING VEGETABLES WITH NOODLES v

FOR 4

3 spring onions, sliced finely

½ inch (1 cm) root ginger, peeled and grated finely

2 cloves garlic, sliced finely

3 oz (75 g) French beans

6 oz (175 g) baby sweetcorn

1 lb (500 g) courgettes

8 oz (250 g) leeks

8 oz (250 g) young carrots

2 tbs vegetable oil

3 tbs soy sauce

1 tbs black bean sauce

2 tbs dark sesame oil

8 oz (250 g) Chinese egg noodles, cooked and drained (or you can use rice noodles)

6 oz (175 g) firm tofu, cut into cubes and browned in olive oil (optional)

2 tbs sesame seeds

A quick supper dish, with fresh flavours and appetizing spicing. Stir-fries make healthy, nutritious meals which you can vary widely, using different vegetables and herbs in season. Vegans can make this using plain noodles.

METHOD: Prepare the spring onions, ginger and garlic. Trim all the vegetables and slice them finely, diagonally.

Heat the oil in a wok and add all the prepared vegetables plus the spring onions, ginger and garlic. Stir-fry briskly together for 4–5 minutes. Add the soy sauce and black bean sauce and stir-fry for a further 2 minutes, then cover and cook gently for 5 minutes or until all the vegetables are tender but still slightly crisp.

Add the dark sesame oil. Add the cooked noodles and the browned tofu, if using, and toss to mix with the vegetables. Sprinkle with the sesame seeds, and serve immediately.

STIR-FRYING

A quick, easy and tasty way of cooking vegetables, this is best done in a wok, but failing that you can use a large frying pan. Cut your fresh vegetables into bite-size pieces, diagonally if you prefer; in some cases they need to be shredded or sliced finely and this can be done very quickly in the food processor.

Heat a very little oil in your wok or pan and smear it over the surface. Groundnut oil is excellent for stir-frying because it is tasteless and doesn't burn easily. Get the oil – and the pan – really hot before you toss in the vegetables, letting the heat sear them as you stir them in the pan. When they are evenly heated through and beginning to cook, turn the heat down a little and stir and toss constantly until they are tender but still crisp. At this point add any other seasonings. In some recipes you then turn the heat right down, cover with a lid and allow the vegetables to steam to a finish. Always serve stir-fried vegetables immediately as they are at their best crisp and hot.

BEST VEGETABLE PAELLA

FOR 4–6

1 oz (25 g) margarine

2 tbs vegetable oil

1 large Spanish onion, chopped

12 oz (350 g) long-grain rice

1½ pints (900 ml) vegetable stock

large pinch of saffron strands, soaked in a little stock

4 cloves garlic, chopped

6 oz (175 g) frozen peas, thawed

2 canned pimientos, chopped, or 1 large fresh red pepper, skinned and chopped

6 oz (175 g) button mushrooms, quartered

4 large tomatoes, skinned and chopped (fresh or canned)

8 oz (250 g) cooked artichoke hearts, halved

6 oz (175 g) mangetout, steamed and sliced diagonally

4 oz (125 g) canned water chestnuts, drained and sliced

sea salt and freshly ground black pepper

finely grated cheese to hand around

This great classic dish from Spain is an eye-catching meal for special occasions.
The traditional fish is replaced by mushrooms, artichoke hearts, mangetout and water chestnuts.
The subtle flavour of saffron permeates the dish and gives it its lovely golden colour. Serve with a watercress salad and fresh, warm bread.

METHOD: Heat the margarine and oil in a large pan or wok. Add the chopped onion and cook over a gentle heat for about 10 minutes or until soft and translucent. Add the rice and cook over moderate heat, stirring constantly, for a couple of minutes. Then begin to add the stock, a little at a time, and simmer until each addition is absorbed. After about 10 minutes, add the saffron and the garlic. Continue cooking for 5 minutes or so or until the rice is tender. Then stir in the rest of the ingredients and stir until heated through. Check the seasoning and serve, with grated cheese to hand around.

SKINNING PEPPERS

Cut peppers into quarters and deseed. Cut each quarter into two or three strips and place skin-side up under a hot grill. Grill for 5–6 minutes or until the skin has blistered and blackened. Remove, place in a brown paper bag and cool. The skin will peel off easily.

SKINNING TOMATOES

Put tomatoes into a large bowl and cover with boiling water. Leave to stand for about 5 minutes. Lift out one by one and pierce the skin with a sharp knife; the skin will peel off easily.

MUSHROOM MOUSSAKA

FOR 6

2 medium aubergines, sliced

5 tbs olive oil

sea salt and freshly ground
black pepper

1 large onion, sliced

1 clove garlic, crushed

1½ lb (750g) flat mushrooms,
or wild mushrooms if
available, sliced

1 x 14oz (400g) can
tomatoes, drained and
chopped, or 6 large fresh
tomatoes, skinned (see page
36) and chopped

1 tbs balsamic vinegar or
fresh lemon juice

4 tbs chopped parsley

1 tbs each chopped fresh
marjoram and thyme

1¼ lb (625g) potatoes, peeled
and boiled 'al dente', then
sliced

8oz (250g) vegetarian mince
browned in 1 tbs vegetable oil
(optional)

2oz (50g) ricotta cheese

¾ pint (450ml) béchamel
sauce (see page 85)

2 tbs grated Cheddar cheese

A great dish for a supper party. Serve with your
favourite rice dish and a seasonal salad
such as the rocket and spinach salad on page 76.
Add a basket of crusty bread and a bottle of retsina –
and transport yourselves to the Mediterranean!

METHOD: Brush the aubergine slices with 3 tbs of the
olive oil and sprinkle them with salt. Arrange in a single
layer on a baking tray and bake at 180°C/350°F/gas 4 for
15 minutes.

In a large pan heat the rest of the olive oil and soften the
onion and garlic, covered, for 10 minutes over a medium to
low heat. Stir occasionally. Then add the mushrooms and
toss thoroughly. Cook, partially covered with a lid, until
they have softened. Add the chopped tomatoes, vinegar or
lemon juice, parsley, marjoram and thyme and mix well.
Season to taste with sea salt and freshly ground black
pepper. Simmer for 5 minutes.

Make a layer of the potato slices in the bottom of a
shallow baking dish. Continue making layers with the
aubergines, mushroom mixture, remaining potatoes and
optional vegetarian mince. Finish with aubergines. Press
down. Stir the ricotta into the béchamel until well blended
and spoon evenly over the surface. Sprinkle with the grated
cheese. Bake at 180°C/ 350°F/gas 4 for 40–45 minutes.

WILD MUSHROOMS

*There is a wonderful choice of wild mushrooms if you wish to harvest
your own from the woods and fields. Chanterelles, puffballs, morels,
boletus and field mushrooms all have unique flavours which are
superb in a variety of recipes. Always take a good field guide with
you, however, to make sure you have picked the right mushroom. A
few wild mushrooms are poisonous.*

CRISPY MUSHROOM LAYERS v

FOR 4–6

6oz (175g) wholemeal breadcrumbs

4oz (125g) chopped nuts

3oz (75g) margarine

1 large onion, chopped finely

10oz (300g) mushrooms, sliced

1 x 14oz (400g) can tomatoes, drained and chopped

2 cloves garlic, crushed

2 tsp dried mixed herbs

sea salt and freshly ground black pepper

Layers of a crisp crumb and nut mixture surround a garlicky mushroom filling. Delicious!

METHOD: Mix the crumbs and nuts together. Melt 2 oz (50g) of the margarine and fry this mixture until golden.

Melt the rest of the margarine in another pan, add the onion, cover and cook over a low heat for 5–8 minutes or until soft. Add the mushrooms and toss thoroughly, then cover and cook gently for 3–4 minutes. Add the tomatoes, garlic and herbs, stir well and season to taste.

Make a layer of half of the breadcrumb mixture on the bottom of a baking dish and place the mushroom filling on top. Finish with a layer of the remaining crumb mixture. Bake at 190°C/375°F/ gas 5 for 30 minutes or until crisp and golden. Serve piping hot.

QUICK MEATLESS STROGANOFF

FOR 4–6

2oz (50g) margarine

2 onions, sliced

2 tbs plain flour

¼ pint (150ml) vegetable stock

½ pint (300ml) white wine

8oz (250g) small mushrooms, cut in half

2 tbs olive oil

8oz (250g) vegetarian steak chunks

½ pint (300ml) soured cream

freshly ground black pepper

chopped parsley to garnish

This is sensational: a great classic recipe adapted for people who prefer to eat a meatless diet. An amazing dish with wonderful flavours – lighter and even more epicurean than the original!

METHOD: Heat the margarine in a saucepan and cook the onions, covered, until soft. Add the flour and stir it in well, then stir in the stock followed by the white wine. Add the mushrooms. Simmer gently, uncovered, for about 5 minutes, stirring occasionally.

Meanwhile, heat the oil and toss the steak chunks until browned all over. Mix them into the mushroom sauce. Stir in the soured cream, season with lots of pepper and cook very gently (without boiling) for 6–8 minutes. Serve sprinkled with chopped parsley.

SUMMER STEW WITH VEGETABLES ▾

FOR 4

1 large onion, sliced

1 large clove garlic, sliced

2 tbs olive oil

1 baby turnip, cubed

6oz (175g) young carrots, sliced

6oz (175g) new potatoes, washed and diced

6oz (175g) cauliflower florets

8oz (250g) baby courgettes, sliced

1 pint (600ml) vegetable stock

2 heaped tbs cornflour, mixed with 3 tbs water

1 x 14oz (400g) can chopped tomatoes with juice

3-4 tbs chopped fresh parsley, thyme, tarragon or other mixed herbs

optional spices, to taste

sea salt and freshly ground pepper

3 tbs vegetable oil

8oz (250g) vegetarian steak chunks

A satisfying stew for people who don't want to eat meat but still like its texture.
You can, of course, vary the vegetables – for a more exotic combination try okra, broccoli, runner or French beans, aubergines and peppers.
You can alter the spicing too, to your taste, adding mace or chilli for example.

METHOD: In a large pan, soften the onion and garlic in the olive oil, covered, over a low heat. Then add the prepared vegetables and brown for 5–6 minutes, stirring and turning. Gradually add the stock, stirring, and bring to the boil, then stir in the cornflour and water mixture. Add the tomatoes with their juice and stir well. Add the herbs, plus any spices that you choose. Season to taste. Turn the heat right down and cover the pan tightly. Simmer gently for 25 minutes, stirring occasionally.

Meanwhile heat the vegetable oil in a shallow pan and brown the steak chunks all over for about 3 minutes. Stir the steak chunks into the stew, cover again and cook gently for a further 10 minutes. Check the seasoning, and it is ready to serve.

SPINACH PANCAKES WITH MUSHROOMS

FOR 4 (Makes 8)

4oz (125g) plain flour

sea salt and freshly ground black pepper

1 free-range egg, beaten

½ pint (300ml) skimmed or soya milk

6oz (175g) cooked spinach (from 14oz/400g fresh), thoroughly drained (squeeze in your hands to remove excess water)

vegetable oil

1oz (25g) margarine

1¼ lb (625g) mushrooms, sliced thinly

3 large cloves garlic, crushed

1oz (25g) plain flour

3fl oz (75ml) skimmed or soya milk

grated nutmeg

4oz (125g) mozzarella cheese, diced

parsley to garnish

Although this takes a little time to prepare, it is well worth the work! The spinach pancakes are wrapped around a garlicky mushroom filling, and finished off in the oven with a topping of melting mozzarella. A lovely supper dish, served with a sauce of your choice plus steamed vegetables and a fennel salad (see page 78).

METHOD: Sift the flour and seasonings into the blender, add the egg and milk and blend until smooth. Add the spinach and blend again. Thin out the batter if necessary with more milk – the consistency depends on the amount of water in the spinach.

Brush an 8 inch (20cm) frying pan with oil, heat it, then add 2 ladles-full of the pancake batter. Spread it to cover the bottom of the pan evenly. Cook the pancake for 1 minute before turning to brown the other side. Keep it warm while you cook the remaining pancakes.

Heat the margarine in another pan and cook the mushrooms with the garlic for 3–4 minutes or until the juices run. Stir in the flour to soak them up, then gradually add the milk a little at a time, stirring so that the sauce is smooth. Season to taste with salt, pepper and nutmeg.

Fill the pancakes with the mushroom mixture, roll them up and place in a baking dish. Scatter the mozzarella over the top and bake at 180°C/350°F/gas 4 for 15 minutes. Serve hot garnished with parsley.

PASTA, RICE AND POTATOES

PASTA, RICE AND POTATOES ARE MAJOR CORNERSTONES OF THE MEATLESS DIET, PROVIDING CARBOHYDRATE BALANCE TO THE VEGETABLE INGREDIENTS AS WELL AS SATISFYING BULK. THEY ARE ENDLESSLY VERSATILE, AND CAN BE USED TO MAKE MAIN MEALS AS WELL AS SIDE DISHES. THEY ARE CHEAP, TOO, AND ALWAYS AVAILABLE.

SPAGHETTINI WITH SUN-DRIED TOMATOES, AUBERGINES AND CHILLI

FOR 4

4 shallots, sliced finely

2 cloves garlic, sliced finely

2 tbs olive oil

1 medium aubergine, cut into small cubes

1 tsp dried mixed herbs

3 oz (75 g) sun-dried tomatoes in oil, sliced

1-2 fresh chillies (according to taste), deseeded and sliced very finely

7 fl oz (200 ml) crème fraîche or single cream

12 oz (350 g) spaghettini

sea salt

grated cheese to hand around

Using fine spaghetti adds finesse to this recipe, but you can also use Japanese buckwheat noodles. Like spaghettini they are very fine, but flat, and their flavour is gorgeous. The bite of chilli in the sauce is an inspired contrast to the softness of the aubergine.

METHOD: Cook the shallots and garlic in the oil, covered, for 5–6 minutes or until soft. Stir in the aubergine and cook for 2–3 minutes. Add the herbs, sun-dried tomatoes and chillies and stir well to mix. Turn the heat down to very low, cover again and steam for 10 minutes, stirring occasionally. Then add the crème fraîche or single cream and heat through for a further 5 minutes. At the same time, cook the spaghettini until 'al dente' (see page 46).

Purée the aubergine mixture in a blender or food processor, or mash to a paste, and season to taste with salt.

Toss the sauce into the hot, well-drained spaghettini and serve immediately, with grated cheese to hand around.

PENNE WITH TOMATOES AND MOZZARELLA

FOR 4

2 tbs olive oil

3 tbs fresh basil, torn into small pieces

6 fresh tomatoes, cut into small squares

6oz (175g) mozzarella cheese, cut into small squares

8 sun-dried tomatoes in oil, chopped (optional)

sea salt and freshly ground black pepper

12oz (350g) penne

This fresh tomato sauce takes only minutes to prepare and is best made with full-flavoured vine-ripened tomatoes in season. The dish goes beautifully with a crisp green salad or the shredded courgette salad on page 77.

METHOD: Put the oil, basil, tomatoes, mozzarella and optional sun-dried tomatoes into a bowl. Season to taste with salt and lots of freshly ground pepper. Leave to stand while you prepare the pasta.

Cook the penne until it is 'al dente' (see below) and drain well. Toss the hot pasta in the sauce until well mixed and serve at once.

HOW TO COOK PASTA

1. Bring water (3¹/₂ pints/2 litres per 8oz/250g pasta) to the boil with 1 tsp olive oil in a large pan and add a generous pinch of sea salt.

2. Put the pasta into the water and bring back to the boil. Simmer over a moderate heat for the shortest cooking time recommended on the packet. Stir from time to time. Alternatively, put the pasta into the boiling water and bring back to the boil, then remove the pan from the heat and cover with a lid. Leave to stand off the heat for the cooking time recommended on the packet, stirring from time to time.

3. To test the pasta, lift out a piece on a long-handled fork or slotted spoon: it is done when it is tender but still firm to the bite ('al dente'). Never overcook pasta.

4. Drain it in a colander, shaking well to remove all excess water. Serve immediately.

RICE NOODLES WITH BROCCOLI, GINGER AND GARLIC v

FOR 6

1 lb (500 g) rice vermicelli

2½ lb (1.25 kg) broccoli florets

For the sauce:

4 spring onions, sliced very finely

1 inch (2.5 cm) fresh root ginger, peeled and grated very finely

2-3 large cloves garlic, crushed

3 tbs black bean sauce

1 tbs soy sauce or to taste

6 tbs dark sesame oil

The combination of ginger and garlic gives a classic oriental flavour to this quick and easy supper dish. You can buy black bean sauce and dark sesame oil from oriental grocers – they are useful standbys to have on the larder shelf.

METHOD: To make the sauce, mix all the ingredients together and leave to stand while you cook the broccoli and vermicelli.

Cover the rice vermicelli with cold water in a large saucepan. Bring to the boil, then remove from the heat and leave to soak for 5 minutes. Meanwhile, steam the broccoli florets and cut them small.

Drain the vermicelli thoroughly and toss with the broccoli florets and the prepared sauce.

STEAMING

Cooking vegetables in a steamer conserves their valuable vitamins and minerals, and retains their full flavour. Vegetables can be steamed either whole, sliced or chopped. Time allowed depends on the size and type of vegetable, and whether you wish to cook them to softness or 'al dente' (slightly crisp). Steamers can be bought at all good kitchen shops.

Cooking vegetables in a microwave oven is also in effect steaming them: covered with film wrap, and with a little water added, this method also brings out the full flavour of the vegetables whilst retaining their goodness.

SUMMER LASAGNE

FOR 6

2 lb (1 kg) small courgettes, steamed lightly and sliced

sea salt and freshly ground black pepper

large bunch of fresh basil, chopped

8 oz (250 g) cottage, ricotta, feta or soft goat's cheese, sliced if necessary

8 oz (250 g) no-cook lasagne

½ pint (300 ml) béchamel sauce (see page 85)

¼ pint (150 ml) crème fraîche or single cream

2 oz (50 g) cheese, grated

3 free-range egg yolks

For the light tomato sauce:

2 tbs olive oil

1 small onion, chopped finely

2 tsp plain flour

2 lb (1 kg) ripe tomatoes, skinned (see page 36) and chopped, or equivalent canned chopped tomatoes

small bunch of fresh herbs, chopped finely

1 inch (2.5 cm) strip of orange rind (optional)

sea salt to taste

Good any time of year, but especially good made when the tomato crop is at its height, and courgettes and basil are at their best. The cheese melts between layers of vegetables and pasta and is mouthwatering. Great served with a seasonal salad and fresh bread.

METHOD: First make the tomato sauce. Heat the oil in a saucepan, add the onion and cook over a low heat, covered, for 8–10 minutes or until softened. Stir in the flour and cook gently, uncovered, for 3 minutes. Stir in the rest of the sauce ingredients. Cover the pan again and simmer for 5 minutes, then remove the lid and simmer for a further 20 minutes, stirring occasionally. Add a little water as necessary to prevent the sauce from sticking (the finished consistency should be quite thick). Discard the orange rind.

Moisten the bottom of an ovenproof dish with a little tomato sauce. Make a layer of sliced courgettes and season with salt and pepper. Sprinkle some chopped basil over them. Cover with slices of cheese and moisten with a little more tomato sauce. Cover with strips of lasagne. Continue making these layers until all the ingredients are used up, ending with a layer of lasagne.

Heat the béchamel gently and stir in the crème fraîche or single cream. Mix in the grated cheese until it melts, and season to taste. Off the heat, beat in the free-range egg yolks. Pour the sauce over the top lasagne layer and bake at 190°C/375°F/gas 5 for 1–1¼ hours or until the topping is deep golden and set.

SPINACH FETTUCCINE WITH CREAMY TOMATOES AND BASIL

FOR 3–4

1 x 14oz (400g) can chopped tomatoes with their juice, or 12oz (350g) fresh tomatoes, skinned (see page 36) and chopped

2 tbs olive oil

3 cloves garlic, sliced finely

large bunch of fresh basil, chopped roughly

sea salt and freshly ground black pepper

½ pint (300ml) crème fraîche or single cream

8oz (250g) spinach fettuccine

2oz (50g) Cheddar cheese, finely grated

This is a pasta dish you can run up in next to no time. Serve with French or Italian bread and a tossed green salad or the roasted pepper salad on page 80.

METHOD: Mix the tomatoes with the olive oil, garlic and basil, and season to taste with salt and pepper. Heat very gently so the flavours blend together, then add the crème fraîche or single cream and stir until smoothly blended. Leave to warm over the lowest possible heat.

Cook the spinach fettuccine until 'al dente' (see page 90) and drain thoroughly. Toss with the sauce. Add the grated Cheddar and toss again. Serve with more grated cheese to hand around.

FRESH AND HOME-DRIED HERBS

When herbs are in season – from late spring through summer – they can be used to impart wonderful flavours and fragrances to food. Fresh herbs make a distinct difference to cooked dishes, and they are delicious in salads. When fresh herbs are out of season or unavailable, dried herbs are an excellent substitute for fresh in soups, casseroles and meatless dishes.

If you grow your own herbs you can dry them quite successfully yourself. Pick them in the morning when they are at the height of their fragrance. You can then either lay them on paper in a warm place to dry out, or tie them into small bunches and hang them in a warm, dry place with plenty of air circulating around them. When brittle – after several days – strip them off their stalks and store in dark jars out of direct sunlight.

MEXICAN RICE 'N' BEANS ⱽ

FOR 2–3

1 x 14oz (400g) can kidney bean or black beans, drained (or equivalent cooked dried, see page 106)

1 large onion, chopped

2 large cloves garlic, sliced

2oz (50g) margarine

1 tbs wholemeal flour

2 tsp ground cumin or to taste

1/2–1 tsp chilli powder

1/2 pint (300ml) vegetable stock

3oz (75g) long-grain rice, cooked (see page 52)

So easy to make, this is hot and tasty, an interesting alternative to beans on toast – and just as nutritious. Provide Tabasco sauce for those who like their Mexican food REALLY hot!

METHOD: In a saucepan mix the beans with the onion and garlic. Using a fork, mix the margarine, flour and spices to a paste. Pour the vegetable stock over the beans, add the spice paste and heat gently, stirring, until smoothly blended. Simmer, uncovered and stirring from time to time, for 30 minutes or until the sauce thickens like gravy.

Arrange the hot cooked rice around the edge of a shallow serving dish and pour the beans into the centre. Serve at once, with Tabasco to hand around.

SIMPLE SAFFRON RICE ⱽ

FOR 4

6oz (175g) basmati rice

2 tbs olive oil

2 fresh red chillies, deseeded and sliced finely (optional)

3 cardamom pods, split open

1-2 tsp cumin seeds

3oz (75g) frozen peas, thawed

pinch of saffron strands soaked in 2 tbs water, drained

sea salt

1 cinnamon stick, bruised

2oz (50g) cashew nuts, browned lightly under the grill

Saffron yellow adds visual appeal to the flavour of the spices in this rice dish, and toasted cashew nuts provide a contrasting crunch.

METHOD: Rinse the rice and cook it until tender (see page 52). Meanwhile, heat the oil and toss the sliced chillies, cardamom pods and cumin seeds for about 2 minutes or until they give out their aromas.

Toss the spice mixture, peas and saffron into the drained hot rice and season with a little salt. Place the cinnamon stick in the centre and sprinkle the toasted cashew nuts over to garnish.

SPANISH RICE Ⓥ

FOR 4

1 large onion, sliced finely

2 tbs olive oil

3 stalks celery, sliced

6oz (175g) frozen peas, cooked and drained

1 fresh chilli, deseeded and sliced finely (to taste)

1 x 14oz (400g) can chopped tomatoes with juice, or 6 fresh tomatoes, skinned (see page 36) and chopped

garam masala

sea salt and freshly ground black pepper

6oz (175g) long-grain rice, cooked (see page 52)

Speed and simplicity are the keynotes here. The spicy vegetable mixture can be cooked in the time it takes to boil the rice. This is a dish likely to be a regular favourite at any time of the year.

METHOD: Cook the onion in the oil over a gentle heat, covered with a lid and stirring occasionally, for 8–10 minutes or until softened.

Stir in the celery over a moderate heat, then add the peas and sliced chilli and mix in well. Heat through, then add the chopped tomatoes and cook for 5 minutes. Season to taste with garam masala, salt and pepper.

Stir into the hot cooked rice and it is ready to serve.

TYPES OF RICE

LONG-GRAIN – *is the most versatile and popular of all types and comes white or brown.*

SHORT-GRAIN – *is often used for risottos and puddings and is usually white. If you can find brown short-grain rice, use it to make delicious, slightly more crunchy risottos.*

BROWN RICE – *is the best rice in nutritional terms: the whole natural grain still with its edible husk, which makes it high in dietary fibre. It has a delicious flavour and nutty texture. Brown rice, both long-grain and short-grain, needs a little more water and longer cooking than white rice.*

BASMATI – *is a narrow long-grain rice variety with a fabulous flavour, great with Indian food. It comes brown or white. Grown in India and Italy.*

ARBORIO – *from Italy, is a plump short-grain rice with good flavour. It makes excellent risottos.*

'PUDDING' RICE – *is polished short-grain rice that goes mushy when cooked because of its high starch content. Perfect for a creamy rice pudding.*

WILD RICE – *is not a true rice at all, but the seed of a water grass. It is long and narrow, grey-brown in colour and nutty in flavour. Wild rice requires longer cooking than other rice – 30-40 minutes – but is nice to mix into rice dishes for variety. I always add a handful of wild rice to long-grain rice.*

RICE FLOUR – *is a good thickening agent in sauces and stews, and can be used in baking. Invaluable for people with a gluten allergy.*

VEGETARIAN MINCE AND RICE STIR-FRY ⓥ

FOR 4

2 tbs olive oil

1 large onion, chopped finely

6oz (175g) vegetarian mince

6oz (175g) long-grain rice, cooked (see below)

1 tbs chopped fresh parsley or other herbs

1 tbsp tomato purée, or 1 x 8oz (250g) can chopped tomatoes

sea salt and freshly ground black pepper

Serve this quick supper dish with a green vegetable such as lemon green beans (see page 28) or a crunchy vegetable salad.

METHOD: Heat the oil in a wok or frying pan and sauté the onion for 5 minutes. Add the mince and stir-fry for 5 minutes or until lightly browned. Stir in the rice, herbs and tomato purée or tomatoes. Season to taste. Heat through, stirring.

HOW TO COOK RICE

There is a simple ratio of 1 to 2 when cooking rice: to one measure of rice you add two measures of water. So weigh the amount of rice required in the recipe, and put it into a cup or measuring jug. You will need two of the cups or measuring jugs full of water to cook the rice.

1. *Rinse rice before you cook it. Then put it into a saucepan, add the measured water and bring to the boil.*

2. *Turn the heat down and cover with a lid so that the pan is sealed. Leave the rice to cook, covered all the time, until it has absorbed all the water. This takes 8-10 minutes for white rice, or up to 20 minutes for brown or risotto rice.*

3. *Add some salt if you wish and fluff up the rice with a fork.*

RICE AND VEGETABLE CHEESE BAKE

FOR 6

1 onion, sliced

3 tbs olive oil

3 courgettes, cubed

1 yellow pepper, deseeded and cut into small squares

6oz (175g) sweetcorn

1 tsp each turmeric, ground cumin and ground ginger

sea salt and freshly ground black pepper

8oz (250g) brown long-grain rice, cooked (see opposite)

4oz (125g) Cheddar cheese, grated

2 free-range eggs, beaten

1oz (25g) margarine

Mixed vegetables spiced with turmeric, cumin and ginger are folded into rice with cheese. The full flavour of this bake goes beautifully with the roasted pepper salad on page 80 or steamed green vegetables.

METHOD: Soften the onion in the oil for 5 minutes over a gentle heat, covered with a lid. Stir in the other vegetables and toss to mix, then cover the pan again and cook for about 10 minutes or until all the vegetables are tender, stirring from time to time. Stir in the spices and season with salt and pepper. Mix into the cooked rice with the grated cheese, and fold in the beaten eggs.

Spread the mixture in an ovenproof dish and dot the top with the margarine. Cover the dish with foil and bake at 180°C/350°F/gas 4 for 40–45 minutes. Allow to rest for 10 minutes before serving, with a cheese and parsley sauce.

CHEESE AND PARSLEY SAUCE

MAKES 3/4 pint (450 ml)

1½ oz (40g) margarine

2 tbs plain flour

1 tbs mild mustard

¼ pint (150ml) skimmed milk

2oz (50g) grated cheese

medium bunch of parsley, chopped finely

¼ pint (150 ml) crème fraîche or single cream (or more milk)

freshly ground black pepper

This popular sauce goes wonderfully well with the cheese bake above. Its flavours also complement pasta dishes.

METHOD: Melt the margarine in a heavy-bottomed saucepan and stir in the flour. When well mixed, stir in the mustard. Slowly add the milk, stirring all the time so that the sauce becomes smooth and thick. Add the grated cheese and the parsley and cook gently for 5 minutes. Add the cream or extra milk, stir until completely smooth, and season to taste with black pepper.

POTATO AND AUBERGINE CURRY ⓥ

FOR 3-4

1 tsp chilli powder

½ tsp turmeric

2 tsp ground cumin or to taste

1 tsp ground coriander or to taste

1 tsp sea salt

1 tbs tomato purée

4 tbs vegetable oil

1 lb (500g) aubergines, sliced

1-2 tsp cumin seeds

1 inch (2.5cm) root ginger, peeled and grated

1 fresh green chilli, deseeded and finely chopped

1 x 7oz (200g) can chopped tomatoes, or 3 large fresh tomatoes, skinned (see page 36) and chopped

4 medium potatoes, boiled and cut into cubes

6oz (175g) vegetarian steak chunks, browned in a little oil (optional)

fresh coriander leaves to garnish

A beautifully spiced potato dish. Serve with basmati rice, some naan bread, and shredded lettuce with a vinaigrette dressing.

METHOD: Mix the spices, salt and tomato purée with 1 tbs of the oil in a small bowl. Spread the spice mixture over the cut sides of the aubergine slices. Cut the slices into strips.

Heat the remaining oil in a frying pan and fry the cumin seeds until they begin to pop. Add the aubergines and grated ginger and turn the heat down. Cover and cook for 8 minutes, stirring once or twice.

Add the chopped chilli, tomatoes and potatoes with 3-4 tbs water and simmer very gently, covered tightly, for 15-20 minutes, stirring from time to time.

Add the browned steak chunks, if using, and mix well. Serve garnished with coriander leaves.

SCALLOPED POTATOES

FOR 3–4

1½ lb (750g) potatoes, peeled and sliced very thinly

3oz (75g) margarine

4 tbs finely chopped fresh chives, spring onions or leeks

4 tbs finely diced red pepper (optional)

sea salt and paprika

1 tsp Dijon mustard (optional)

½ pint (300ml) skimmed or soya milk

single cream (optional)

1-2oz (25-50g) Cheddar cheese, grated

This simple potato dish is a classic that you can vary by using all kinds of herbs and vegetables in between the layers of potato.

METHOD: Make layers of the potatoes in a shallow baking dish, with tiny knobs of margarine, the chives, spring onions or leeks, and optional peppers between them. Sprinkle each layer with sea salt and paprika as you go. Mix the mustard with a little milk, then add to the rest of the milk, with some cream if you like. Pour over the top of the layered potatoes and sprinkle with the grated cheese.

Bake at 180°C/350°F/gas 4 for 1½ hours, covered with foil for the first 30 minutes.

STUFFED BAKED POTATOES

FOR 4–6

4 large baking potatoes, scrubbed

½ pint (300ml) béchamel sauce (see page 85)

4oz (125g) Cheddar cheese, grated, plus more for the tops

4oz (125g) cooked peas

4oz (125g) cooked carrots, diced small

A nice change from plain jacket baked potatoes. You can vary the vegetables – chopped onions or leeks, sliced mushrooms, diced peppers and sweetcorn would all be delicious.

METHOD: Bake the potatoes at 200°C/400°F/gas 6 for 1¼ hours or until tender. Cut in half lengthwise and remove the flesh, being careful not to break the skins. Mash the flesh in a bowl and set the skins aside.

Heat the béchamel gently and stir in the grated cheese until it melts. Mix into the potato, then fold in the vegetables. Fill the skins with the mixture. Cover with grated cheese and bake for 6–8 minutes or until the tops are light brown.

SAVOURY FRIED POTATO ⱽ

FOR 2–4

1 lb (500 g) mashed potatoes

plain flour

sea salt

freshly ground black pepper

vegetable oil

margarine

This is a delicious way to use up left-over mash!
You can vary the recipe with sautéed
mushrooms, leeks or onions, or grated cheese.

METHOD: Divide the mashed potatoes into 4 or 8 equal portions and shape each into a cake with floured hands. (If the potatoes are moist you will need to mix a bit of flour into them to help bind the cakes.) Season some flour and use to coat the cakes lightly.

Heat a mixture of oil and margarine in a frying pan and fry the cakes over a moderate heat until crisp and golden brown on both sides. Serve hot.

ROSTI ⱽ

FOR 4

2 lb (1 kg) potatoes, peeled

sea salt and freshly ground black pepper

2 tbs olive oil

1 oz (25 g) margarine

Serve this as a supper dish with a salad,
or as a side dish.

METHOD: Grate the potatoes coarsely. Press dry between sheets of kitchen paper and season well.

Heat the oil with the margarine in a heavy-bottomed frying pan over a high heat. Add the potatoes and flatten into a cake. Turn the heat down, cover tightly with a lid and cook gently for 25–30 minutes or until the base of the rosti is crusty and browned and the top is tender.

To turn out, place a plate over the top of the pan and turn the pan over so that the rosti falls out on to the plate. Serve at once.

PASTRY

PASTRY DISHES ALWAYS LOOK SO APPETIZING – CRISP, GOLDEN AND MOUTHWATERINGLY LIGHT. THIS WONDERFUL SELECTION OF RECIPES DEMONSTRATES JUST HOW VERSATILE PASTRY IS, FROM THE ELEGANT FILO AND PUFF PASTRY TO THE EVER-POPULAR PIZZA.

SAVOURY VEGETABLE STRUDEL

FOR 4–6

1½ oz (40g) margarine, melted

3 tbs olive oil

ten 12 x 6 inch (30 x 15 cm) sheets filo pastry

8 oz (250g) courgettes, steamed and sliced thinly

8 oz (250g) broccoli, steamed and sliced

4 oz (125g) French beans, steamed and cut in half

6 oz (175g) goat's cheese, feta or Cheddar cheese, sliced or crumbled

sea salt and freshly ground black pepper

1 tbs fresh thyme

1 tbs chopped fresh tarragon (optional)

1 free-range egg, beaten

flowers or herbs to garnish

This sensational pastry roll encases lightly cooked vegetables which are bound together with melted cheese. For something so special it is delightfully simple to prepare, and naturally you can experiment by varying the vegetables.

METHOD: Mix the melted margarine with the olive oil. Brush 5 of the filo pastry sheets with the mixture and stack them on top of each other.

Mix the prepared vegetables together with the cheese. Season with salt and pepper and add the thyme and tarragon (if using). Take half of the mixture and spread it over the surface of the stacked pastry, leaving a 2 inch (5 cm) margin clear all around. Fold the short edges in, and roll up from a long side like a Swiss roll. Brush the surface with beaten egg and place seam-side down on a well-greased baking tray. Repeat with the other half of the ingredients to make a second strudel.

Bake at 190°C/375°F/gas 5 for 30–40 minutes or until golden brown and crisp. Leave to stand for a few minutes before slicing, and serve on a warmed dish garnished with flowers or herbs.

VEGETABLE SPRING ROLLS v

MAKES 12

2 tbs groundnut or olive oil plus more for deep frying

12 oz (350 g) mixed vegetables, such as mangetout, peas, broccoli, courgettes, carrots, water chestnuts, all cut very small

5 oz (150 g) button mushrooms, chopped

3 oz (75 g) beansprouts

4 spring onions, chopped finely

2 inches (5 cm) root ginger, peeled and grated

1 clove garlic, chopped finely

2-3 tbs soy sauce

24 sheets filo pastry

Spring rolls are perennial favourites and the home-made variety is unbeatable. Serve these as a starter for a special meal, or as a supper dish for friends, with Spanish rice (see page 51).

METHOD: Heat the groundnut oil and stir-fry (see page 34) all the prepared vegetables with the ginger and garlic. Stir in soy sauce to taste. Remove from the heat, cover and leave to stand for several minutes.

Put 2 tablespoons of the vegetable filling on a single filo sheet and roll it up, tucking in the sides to make a neat parcel. Immediately roll this roll in another sheet of filo. Repeat to make 12 spring rolls in all. Deep-fry in very hot oil (190°C/375°F), turning the spring rolls until they are light golden all over and crisp. Drain on kitchen paper and serve as soon as possible.

PEELING GARLIC

Press down on the clove with the flat side of a knife blade, then pull away the burst skin.

BEST VEGETABLE QUICHE

FOR 6

9oz (275g) easy shortcrust pastry (see page 64)

1¼ lb (625g) small courgettes, sliced thinly

2oz (50g) margarine

2 large cloves garlic, sliced finely

2 tsp garam masala or to taste (optional)

3 free-range eggs

7fl oz (200ml) single cream

sea salt

A quiche is always a winner – a crisp pastry case holding a lovely creamy vegetable filling. The version here uses courgettes. Alternative vegetables include: broccoli florets, sliced or small button mushrooms, thinly sliced leeks, chopped artichoke hearts, cauliflower florets and spinach. Quiches freeze well, so can be a useful standby.

METHOD: Roll out the pastry dough and line a greased 8 inch (20cm) loose-bottomed flan tin. Bake blind until part cooked (see below). Leave to cool.

Sauté the courgettes in the margarine until soft and turning golden brown. Remove from the heat and mix in the garlic and optional garam masala. Beat the eggs thoroughly with the cream and season with a little salt.

Arrange the courgettes in overlapping rings in the pastry case, then carefully pour the cream and egg mixture over the top. Bake at 220°C/425°F/gas 7 for 30 minutes. Cool on a wire rack for at least 10 minutes before lifting the quiche carefully out of the tin.

BAKING BLIND

Baking blind means baking a pastry case before it is filled. If after the filling is put in, the tart, quiche, flan, etc is to be baked further, then the pastry case is baked blind only until it is part cooked. If no further baking is to be done after the filling is added, the pastry case is baked blind until it is completely cooked.

Roll out the pastry dough on a lightly floured board and line the tin. Press the dough lightly into the corners and edges, and trim the edge. Prick with a fork in several places, then spread a piece of foil smoothly over bottom and sides of the pastry case; the foil should overlap the rim of the tin by 2 inches (5cm). Fill with baking beans. (You can buy ceramic baking beans, or simply use dried beans that you keep specially for this purpose.)

Bake at 200°C/400°F/gas 6 for 10-15 minutes or until just set, then remove the beans and foil. Return to the oven (without the foil and beans) and bake for a further 5 minutes to crisp and brown the pastry slightly. The pastry case is now part cooked. To bake completely, return to the oven (without the foil and beans) and bake for a further 15 minutes or until the pastry is firm and golden brown.

Easy leek puffs

MAKES 4

12 oz (350 g) leeks, chopped and cooked

½ pint (300 ml) béchamel sauce (see page 85)

1 oz (25 g) Cheddar cheese, grated

1 lb (500 g) frozen or home-made puff pastry (see page 64)

1 free-range egg yolk, beaten

You can vary the filling for these delectably light puff pastry triangles throughout the seasons – broccoli, courgettes, peas, spinach and mushrooms all make tasty fillings. They are wonderfully easy to make, and a firm favourite whenever they appear.

METHOD: Stir the leeks into the béchamel, mixing thoroughly. Stir in the grated cheese.

Roll out the puff pastry fairly thinly and cut it into four 5 inch (12.5 cm) squares. Moisten the edges with water. Place one-quarter of the leek mixture in the centre of each square. Take one corner and fold it over to the opposite corner. Press the edges of the triangle together with a fork, so that they are well sealed. Brush the tops with beaten egg yolk and place on a well-greased baking tray.

Bake at 220°C/425°F/gas 7 for 20–25 minutes or until risen and golden.

VEGETABLE MILLE-FEUILLES WITH PESTO

FOR 4

1 lb (500g) frozen or home-made puff pastry (see page 64)

1 free-range egg, beaten

For the vegetable filling:

1½ lb (750g) mixed vegetables, eg asparagus, mangetout, broccoli florets, peas, courgettes, sweetcorn, spinach

7 fl oz (200ml) crème fraîche

2 tbs pesto sauce (see page 90)

Mille-feuilles don't necessarily have to be the domain of sweet pâtisserie – savoury ones are wonderful too: elegant, appetizing food that melts in the mouth.

METHOD: Roll the pastry out thinly and cut it into 8 rectangles measuring 2 x 5 inches (5 x 12.5 cm). Brush each one with beaten egg and place on a well-greased baking tray. Bake at 200°C/400°F/gas 6 for 8–10 minutes or until well risen and golden. Split the pastry puffs horizontally about one-third of the way up their height, and keep hot.

Cut the vegetables into short lengths or small cubes and steam them until they are tender but still crisp. Mix together the crème fraîche and pesto and fold in the vegetables so that they are lightly coated. Heat through gently.

Pile the vegetable filling on the bottom layer of each mille-feuille and cover with the top layer of pastry. Serve immediately while crisp.

EASY SHORTCRUST PASTRY ᴠ

MAKES 9 oz (275 g)

3 oz (75 g) margarine

large pinch of fine sea salt

6 oz (175 g) plain flour

3 tbs cold water

METHOD: Put all the ingredients into the blender or food processor and blend until amalgamated and crumbly. Knead to a smooth dough on a floured board, then chill for at least 30 minutes before using.

   If you don't have a blender or food processor, sift the flour with the salt into a bowl and rub in the margarine, lifting the mixture to incorporate as much air as possible. When the mixture resembles fine breadcrumbs, bind with the water. Knead on a floured board until smooth.

PUFF PASTRY ᴠ

MAKES 1 lb (500 g)

8 oz (250 g) plain flour

pinch of salt

8 oz (250 g) margarine

¼ pint (150 ml) ice cold water

squeeze of fresh lemon juice

METHOD: Sift the flour with the salt into a bowl and rub in a walnut-size piece of margarine. Bind with the water and lemon juice and knead to make a smooth dough. Chill for 15 minutes.

   Roll out the dough to an oblong. Place the margarine, in a block, in the centre. Wrap the dough around the margarine like a parcel and turn over. **Roll out to an oblong again, fold in three (the bottom third up and the top third down) and press the side edges to seal them. Give the dough a quarter turn so that these edges are at the top and bottom.** Repeat from ** to **. Wrap in greaseproof paper or a teacloth and chill for 15 minutes. Repeat from ** to ** six more times, chilling between each of these 'turns'. Chill for 10 minutes before rolling out finally for baking. Bake at 220°C/425°F/gas 7.

EASY PIZZA

A home-made pizza is hard to beat, and makes
a satisfying and delicious meal for all the
family. Serve with a simple leafy salad tossed with the
balsamic garlic and herb dressing on page 82.

FOR 4

For the dough:

*scant ¼ oz (5g) easy-blend
yeast*

10oz (300g) plain flour

pinch of salt

*4-5 fl oz (125-150ml) warm
water*

1 tbs olive oil

For the topping:

6 tsp tomato purée

*12oz (350g) ripe tomatoes,
sliced*

1 tbs mixed dried herbs

*sea salt and freshly ground
black pepper*

*optional garnishes: sliced
fresh chilli, red onion rings,
black olives*

*6oz (175g) mozzarella
cheese, sliced, or firm goat's
cheese, grated*

METHOD: To make the dough, mix the yeast with the
flour and salt, and stir in enough warm water to make a soft
dough. Knead thoroughly for 10–15 minutes. Halfway
through this time, add the olive oil.

Press out the dough in a well-greased 11 inch (27.5 cm)
metal pizza plate. Cover with a cloth and leave to rise in a
warm place for 1 hour.

Spread the tomato purée over the dough and arrange the
tomato slices on top. Sprinkle with the herbs, and season
with salt and pepper. If you are using chilli or red onion
rings, scatter them on top. Cover with the cheese and add
olives, if using.

Bake at 220°C/425°F/gas 7 for 20–25 minutes or until the
base is well cooked and the topping browned.

OTHER IDEAS FOR TOPPINGS

- red onions, blue cheese and rosemary
- grilled aubergines and simple pesto ᴠ
- leeks, tomatoes and goat's cheese
- roasted aubergines and mozzarella
- multicolour peppers, tomatoes and mozzarella
- wild mushrooms, garlic and herbs ᴠ
- artichoke hearts, onions and cheese

BARBECUES

EVEN THE MOST COMMITTED OF CARNIVORES WILL ENJOY A MEATLESS BARBECUE, WITH VEGETARIAN SAUSAGES, PATTIES, BURGERS AND HOT DOGS MARINATED IN A BARBECUE SAUCE. THERE ARE PLENTY OF VEGETABLES THAT BARBECUE WELL, SUCH AS AUBERGINES, COURGETTES, MUSHROOMS, POTATOES AND CORN ON THE COB. SERVE WITH SALADS AND LOTS OF TASTY SAUCES, HOME-MADE SALSAS AND DIPS.

CHAR-GRILLED AUBERGINES V

FOR 6

2 large aubergines

olive oil

chopped fresh herbs

sea salt and freshly ground black pepper

Slices of aubergine marinated in herbs and oil take on the flavour of charcoal really well. They turn very soft and are wonderful with crisp barbecued vegetarian sausages and the avocado, mozzarella and tomato salad on page 77.

METHOD: Cut the aubergines diagonally into ½ inch (1cm) slices. Mix the olive oil with herbs, salt and pepper and brush over the cut sides of the aubergine slices. Leave to marinate for up to 1 hour, basting and turning occasionally.

Grill on the rack over hot coals for about 5–6 minutes on each side, until the aubergine is soft and well cooked.

Serve with sauces of your choice (see pages 86-91).

RIGHT: Vegetarian Sausages and Burgers, Char-grilled Aubergines, Courgettes with Herbs and Country Mushrooms

MARINATED VEGETARIAN SAUSAGES AND BURGERS v

FOR 6–8

vegetarian sausages and burgers

barbecue sauce (see page 87)

buns or baps to serve

My piquant, garlicky barbecue sauce is perfect for brushing on to vegetarian sausages and burgers before cooking. For extra flavour, make your fire with mesquite or other aromatic woods, or use a good charcoal.

METHOD: Brush the sausages and burgers with barbecue sauce and leave to marinate if you have the time. Otherwise, just brush with the sauce before cooking.

When the fire is ready, put your sausages and burgers on the grill and brown them, then flip them over and brown the other side. Vegetarian burgers and sausages don't need as long to cook as meat because they are not so tough!

Serve in buns or baps with more barbecue sauce or with any other goodie from this section or others.

CHAR-GRILLED MUSHROOMS WITH ROSEMARY AND GARLIC v

FOR 3–4

8oz (250g) shiitake mushrooms

1 tbs olive oil

1 tbs soy sauce

3 cloves garlic, crushed

1 tsp finely chopped fresh rosemary or ½ tsp dried rosemary

freshly ground black pepper

Mushrooms take on the woody flavour of charcoal exceptionally well, and are always popular as part of a barbecue meal. I've used fresh shiitake mushrooms here, but you could just as easily substitute large button mushrooms

METHOD: Trim the mushroom stalks. Mix the remaining ingredients together, add the mushrooms and toss to coat. Leave to marinate for up to 30 minutes.

Grill on the rack over hot coals for about 3 minutes on each side, and serve hot.

VEGETABLE KEBABS v

FOR 6–8

8oz (250g) medium carrots, cut into chunks

1 small cauliflower, separated into florets

6oz (175g) mangetout, topped and tailed

6oz (175g) baby onions, peeled

3 small corn cobs, cut across into 1 inch (2.5cm) slices

milk or soya milk

vegetarian sausages, burgers, grills etc, cut into chunks (optional)

olive oil

Colourful combinations of vegetables make beautiful kebabs, which you can vary endlessly using peppers of all colours, tomatoes, courgettes etc – whatever is in high season. Serve with a variety of sauces such as barbecue (page 87), chilli (page 88) or roasted red pepper (page 87).

METHOD: Cook all the vegetables separately in boiling water to which you have added 1 tbs milk, until they are tender but still slightly crisp. Drain in a colander under cold running water.

Thread the pieces of vegetable on to skewers, alternating the colours. Include the chunks of vegetarian sausages, etc if you are using them. Brush with oil, and grill on the rack over hot coals for 5 minutes, turning frequently.

GRILLED MARINATED VEGETABLES v

FOR 6

6 large flat mushrooms

3 peppers

6 courgettes, cut in half lengthwise

2 red onions, sliced thickly

¼ pint (150ml) teriyaki sauce

1 clove garlic, crushed

4-5 fresh basil leaves, chopped, or a large pinch of chopped fresh tarragon

Barbecued vegetables are scrumptious, particularly when they are marinated in this Japanese sauce which you can buy in bottles from most large supermarkets.
You can also just brush the vegetables with plenty of olive oil before grilling them.

METHOD: Cut the vegetables into bite-size pieces and thread them on to skewers, alternating the colours. Mix the teriyaki sauce with the garlic and basil or tarragon, add the skewers and leave to marinate for 20–30 minutes.

Put the skewers on the rack over hot coals and grill for about 5 minutes, turning from time to time.

COURGETTES WITH HERBS ▼

FOR 8

8 small courgettes, trimmed

2 cloves garlic, crushed

1 tbs grated fresh ginger

6 fresh mint leaves, chopped finely

1 tsp chopped fresh marjoram

1 tsp chopped fresh lemon verbena or lemon balm

2 dried bay leaves, crumbled

4 tbs fresh lemon juice

3 tbs olive oil

salt

lemon slices and sprigs of fresh herbs to garnish

Small courgettes marinated with herbs, garlic and ginger give out wonderful aromas as they are basted on the barbecue. They go beautifully with barbecued vegetarian sausages, and a watercress salad.

METHOD: Run the tip of a sharp knife along the courgettes to score them.

Mix the garlic, ginger and herbs with the lemon juice and oil and season with a little salt. Turn the courgettes in the mixture until thoroughly coated, then leave to marinate for 4–5 hours, turning occasionally.

Remove the courgettes from the marinade and grill on the rack over hot coals for 8–10 minutes or until tender but still 'al dente'. Turn and baste with the marinade frequently.

Serve skewered on wooden sticks, garnished with lemon slices and sprigs of fresh herbs.

SAGE AND CREAM JACKETS

FOR 6

6 baking potatoes, scrubbed

olive oil

3 tbs white wine vinegar

1 bunch spring onions, sliced finely

1 free-range egg yolk

1 tbs mild mustard

sea salt and freshly ground black pepper

¼ pint (150ml) soured cream

1 tbs finely chopped fresh sage

fresh sage leaves to garnish

Potatoes baked in foil, nestled in the hot coals, have a quality all their own.

METHOD: Rub the potatoes with oil and wrap in double thickness foil. Bake in the hot coals for 45 minutes to 1 hour or until soft, turning occasionally.

To make the sauce, heat the vinegar in a small saucepan with the spring onions until it has almost evaporated. Remove from the heat. Beat together the egg yolk, mustard, salt and pepper, and stir into the pan. Stir in the soured cream and chopped sage and mix well. Keep hot.

Cut a deep cross in the top of each baked potato and squeeze the sides to open them out. Spoon in some sauce and serve garnished with sage leaves.

COUNTRY MUSHROOMS ❣

FOR 6 or 12

¼ pint (150ml) virgin olive oil

4 tbs horseradish sauce

sea salt and freshly ground black pepper

12 flat mushrooms, stalks removed

chopped parsley to garnish

The rustic flavour of horseradish in the marinade permeates the mushrooms in this very simple recipe. Great as part of a large mixed barbecue menu along with vegetable kebabs (see page 69), jacket potatoes and a selection of salads and sauces.

METHOD: Mix together the olive oil and horseradish sauce in a soup plate or shallow dish and season to taste. Add the mushrooms and spoon the liquid over them until they are completely coated. Leave to marinate for a minimum of 30 minutes, basting occasionally.

Grill on the rack over hot coals for about 10 minutes, turning and basting occasionally. Garnish the open sides of the mushrooms with chopped parsley before serving.

CRUSTY GARLIC POTATOES

FOR 4–6

1 lb (500g) new potatoes, scrubbed

3-4 large cloves garlic, peeled

2 free-range eggs, beaten

6-8 tbs yellow cornmeal

sprigs of parsley to garnish

New potatoes stuffed with slivers of garlic and char-grilled with a crust of cornmeal make a very tasty dish to go with barbecued vegetarian burgers and a salad. Delicious with the chilli sauce on page 88.

METHOD: Cook the potatoes in boiling salted water for 12–15 minutes or until tender. Drain and leave to cool slightly. Slice the garlic thickly and, using the tip of a sharp knife or skewer, insert deeply into the potatoes. Dip the potatoes first into beaten egg and then in cornmeal to coat all over.

Grill on the rack over hot coals for 10–15 minutes or until crusty and golden, turning occasionally and taking care that the cornmeal doesn't burn. Serve in a basket lined with a clean napkin, garnished with sprigs of parsley.

PEACHES AND BUTTERSCOTCH

FOR 6 or 12

6 peaches, cut in half and stone removed

2 oz (50g) ground almonds

For the butterscotch sauce:

3 oz (75g) light soft brown sugar

¼ pint (150ml) maple syrup

1½ oz (40g) margarine

pinch of salt

¼ pint (150ml) single cream

1 tsp vanilla essence

METHOD: To make the sauce, combine the sugar, maple syrup, margarine and salt in a heavy-bottomed saucepan. Bring to the boil, stirring to dissolve the sugar, and boil for 3 minutes or until the mixture is thick. Stir in the cream and bring back to the boil, then remove from the heat immediately and stir in the vanilla. Set aside.

Put the peach halves, cut side down, on squares of double thickness foil. Curl the edges of the foil up around the fruit and place on the rack over hot coals. Cook for 5 minutes.

Turn the peach halves over on the foil and spoon the ground almonds into the hollows. Pour 1 tbs of the butterscotch sauce over each half. Carefully draw up the edges of the foil over the top, and seal. Cook over the coals for a further 10 minutes or until tender. Serve hot with the remaining butterscotch sauce.

PRALINE BANANAS ⱽ

FOR 6

½ oz (15 g) shelled almonds

½ oz (15g) shelled hazelnuts

2 oz (50g) granulated sugar

6 under-ripe bananas

METHOD: Put the nuts and sugar in a small heavy-bottomed frying pan and heat gently, stirring until the sugar dissolves. Turn the heat up and cook to a deep brown syrup. Immediately pour on to a sheet of non-stick paper placed on a metal baking sheet on a wooden board. Leave until cold and brittle, then crush finely.

Lay the unpeeled bananas flat and make a slit in the skin along the top. Slightly open out the skin and add about 1 tbs praline to each banana. Wrap up tightly in double-thickness foil and seal along the top. Cook directly on medium-hot coals for 8–10 minutes, turning halfway through the cooking time. Serve in the skins, with whipped cream or thick Greek yogurt.

RIGHT: Peaches and Butterscotch

SALADS

EATING FRESH, RAW INGREDIENTS HAS BEEN SHOWN TO BE BENEFICIAL TO HEALTH, AND IS RECOMMENDED AS PART OF THE DAILY DIET. YOU CAN EAT SALADS AS MAIN MEALS, AS STARTERS OR AS A SIDE DISH. FULL OF VITAMINS AND MINERALS, SALADS GIVE US A FEELING OF VITALITY AND ENERGY THAT MANY OTHER FOODS DO NOT.

WATERCRESS SALAD WITH GARLIC CROUTONS v

FOR 4

2 thick slices of bread, crusts removed

1 clove garlic, cut in half

olive oil for frying

2 bunches of watercress

a handful of crisp lettuce leaves

6 tbs vinaigrette (see page 82)

An elegant combination of watercress and crisp lettuce dressed with vinaigrette, this delectable salad has the added treat of crunchy, garlicky croutons.

METHOD: Cut the bread into small cubes. Rub the cut side of the garlic over the surface of a frying pan, then discard the garlic. Heat enough oil for shallow frying in the pan, about ½ inch (1 cm), and fry the bread gently until golden brown all over. Remove with a slotted spoon and drain on kitchen paper.

Prepare the watercress and lettuce. Line a salad bowl with the lettuce leaves. Toss the watercress in the vinaigrette until well coated. Pile the watercress inside the lettuce leaves and scatter the croutons over the top.

SPICY RAW MUSHROOM SALAD

FOR 3–4

12oz (350g) small button mushrooms

1-2 tsp curry paste

4 tbs mayonnaise

1 tbs fresh lemon juice

1 large clove garlic, crushed (optional)

fresh coriander leaves to garnish

Sliced button mushrooms dressed in a slightly curried mayonnaise and sprinkled with fresh coriander make an excellent starter, as well as a tasty addition to a buffet table.

METHOD: Slice the mushrooms. Mix the curry paste into the mayonnaise with the lemon juice and add the garlic if desired. Fold in the mushrooms and mix thoroughly until they are well coated in the mayonnaise. Put into a serving dish and garnish with fresh coriander leaves.

SPECIAL ROCKET SALAD WITH SPINACH AND PARMESAN

FOR 2–3

5oz (150g) rocket leaves

6oz (175g) young spinach leaves

sea salt

4 tbs extra virgin olive oil

2 tbs fresh lemon juice, or to taste

1½ oz (40g) Parmesan or any favourite cheese, finely shaved or grated

A salad of assertive flavours, this mixture of rocket and spinach in a simple dressing of olive oil and lemon juice makes a wonderful side dish or starter. Cheese shavings scattered over the top give added distinction.

METHOD: Prepare the rocket and spinach leaves, put them in a salad bowl and sprinkle with sea salt. Mix the olive oil with the lemon juice, add to the leaves and toss to coat. Scatter the shavings of Parmesan on top and it is ready to serve.

AVOCADO, MOZZARELLA AND TOMATO SALAD

FOR 4

2 ripe avocados, peeled and stone removed

lemon juice to sprinkle

8oz (250g) mozzarella cheese

1lb (500g) tomatoes

5 tbs vinaigrette (see page 82)

handful of fresh basil leaves

An Italian classic, this is a salad of complementary textures and contrasting rich colours.
It's important to use ripe, full-flavoured tomatoes.
You can serve this as a starter or side salad.

METHOD: Slice the avocados and sprinkle immediately with lemon juice to prevent them from going brown. Slice the mozzarella and tomatoes.

Arrange the slices of green avocado, white cheese and red tomato decoratively in a shallow dish. Drizzle the vinaigrette over the top and scatter the basil leaves over the salad just before serving.

SHREDDED COURGETTE SALAD ♥

FOR 6

4 medium courgettes, trimmed

3 tbs fresh lemon juice

2 tbs extra virgin olive oil

1 medium clove garlic, crushed

1 tbs grated fresh ginger

sea salt and freshly ground black pepper

2 tbs capers

2 tbs pine nuts

A fresh and simple salad for late summer, when courgettes are at their best. Fresh ginger, capers and pine nuts add an unusual piquant note.
Serve with warm garlic bread.

METHOD: Grate the courgettes and pat them dry with kitchen paper. Combine the lemon juice, olive oil, garlic, ginger, salt and pepper in a small jar and shake to blend. Pour the dressing over the courgettes and add the capers and pine nuts. Mix thoroughly and serve immediately. (If left to stand it will go watery.)

CARROT SALAD ⓥ

FOR 4

8 medium carrots, grated

4 tbs chopped parsley

7 spring onions, chopped finely

3 tbs vinaigrette (see page 82)

This salad is utterly simple, yet delicious, nutritious and fresh. If you prefer a slightly stronger bite, you can use a red onion instead of the spring onions.

METHOD: Mix together the carrots, parsley and spring onions in a salad bowl. Dress with the vinaigrette and toss thoroughly to mix well.

FENNEL SALAD

FOR 4–6

12 radishes, trimmed

3 bulbs fennel, trimmed

2 medium carrots, peeled

1 green eating apple, cored

1 tbs fresh lemon juice

6 tbs mayonnaise

This healthy, crunchy salad of fennel, carrot, apple and radish is dressed in a lemony mayonnaise, which adds to its freshness. Food for vitality.

METHOD: Make four vertical cuts, crossing in the centre, in each radish. Soak in iced water for 2–3 hours or until the 'petals' open. Drain.

Cut the fennel bulbs lengthwise in half and cut out the hard core. Slice very finely. Cut the carrots into matchsticks. Dice the apple. Mix the lemon juice into the vegetables, and then toss with the mayonnaise. Pile into a salad bowl and garnish with the radishes.

RIGHT: Carrot Salad and Fennel Salad

PROVENCAL PEPPER SALAD v

FOR 6

1 tbs each finely chopped fresh parsley, tarragon, chervil and chives

1 recipe quantity vinaigrette (see page 82)

2 red peppers

2 green peppers

6 ripe tomatoes, sliced

4 hard-boiled eggs, shelled and sliced, or 1 cubed potato, cooked until just tender

24 black olives

This is a salad redolent of the Mediterranean, with its aromatic fresh herbs.

METHOD: Stir the herbs into the vinaigrette and leave to stand while you prepare the salad.

Skin the red peppers (see page 36) and cut the red and green peppers into long strips. (Green peppers have thinner skin which it is less important to remove.) Place the tomatoes in the bottom of a large, flat serving dish and drizzle one-quarter of the dressing over them. Arrange the pepper strips in a criss-cross pattern on the tomatoes and drizzle with half of the remaining dressing. Cover with the slices of hard-boiled egg and drizzle the rest of the vinaigrette over them. Decorate with olives before serving.

ROASTED PEPPERS WITH MUSHROOMS AND ROCKET v

FOR 4–6

12 oz (350g) small button mushrooms

1 red or yellow pepper, skinned (see page 36) and cut into thick strips

2 tbs capers, drained

¼ pint (150ml) balsamic garlic and herb dressing (see page 82)

2 large handfuls of rocket

8-12 green olives, pitted

Juicy peppers, tender mushrooms and the earthy flavour of rocket combine to make an original salad. The taste of balsamic vinegar in the garlicky dressing adds a special touch.

METHOD: Cut the mushrooms in half, unless they are very tiny. Mix together with the pepper strips and capers, and toss with all but 2 tbs of the dressing. Leave to marinate for 20–30 minutes.

Prepare the rocket and toss with the remaining dressing. Place in the bottom of a salad bowl and arrange the vegetables on top. Garnish with the olives and serve.

RIGHT: Provençal Pepper Salad

VINAIGRETTE v

FOR 4–6

1-2 tsp mild or grainy mustard

2 tbs fresh lemon juice

2 tbs wine vinegar, balsamic vinegar or cider vinegar

sea salt and freshly ground black pepper

5 tbs extra virgin olive oil

crushed garlic to taste (optional)

Here's a recipe for the basic dressing that can be used for almost any salad. Experiment with different oils, vinegars and mustards, to find the combination you like best, and vary the ingredients to suit the salads too.

METHOD: Mix the mustard with the lemon juice and vinegar and season with salt and pepper. Stir in the olive oil gradually so that the dressing thickens as you work. It should become creamy in consistency. Stir in the garlic (if using). Allow to stand for up to 30 minutes before using, to allow the flavours to develop.

BALSAMIC GARLIC AND HERB DRESSING v

MAKES 4 fl oz (125 ml)

3-4 tbs balsamic vinegar

2 cloves garlic, crushed

sea salt and freshly ground black pepper

5 tbs extra virgin olive oil

1 tbs chopped parsley

1 tsp chopped fresh tarragon, basil or any combination of favourite herb

METHOD: Mix the balsamic vinegar with the garlic and seasoning to taste. Gradually add the olive oil, whisking all the time so that the dressing amalgamates thoroughly. Whisk in the fresh herbs.

KEEPING SALAD FRESH

Cut or torn salad leaves, washed and dried in a salad spinner, will keep crisp longer if they are stored in an airtight bag in the refrigerator.

SOY AND LEMON DRESSING ♥

MAKES ¼ **pint (150 ml)**

juice of 1 lemon

3-4 tbs soy sauce

6 tbs dark sesame oil

1 tsp grated fresh ginger

1 clove garlic, crushed

freshly ground black pepper

A tangy dressing with an Oriental flavour

METHOD: Place the lemon juice, soy sauce, sesame oil, ginger, garlic and pepper in a small bowl. Whisk until well blended and use immediately.

FLOWER GARNISHES

Many common flowers, both garden and wild, are edible. They make great additions to salads, or can be used as stuffing garnishes. When your herbs flower in spring and early summer add the flowers to your salads along with the chopped leaves. Lovely scented rose petals can be used as the summer progresses.

You can also choose from the following:

allium, apple blossoms, carnations and pinks, courgette, cornflowers, daisies, geraniums, gladioli, hawthorn, honeysuckle, hop flowers, hibiscus, jasmine, lavender, lilac, lime flowers, mallow, marigolds, nasturtiums, pansies, pea flowers, plum blossoms, radish flower, rosemary, snapdragons, stocks, strawberry flowers and violets.

SAUCES AND DIPS

A GOOD SAUCE WILL ENHANCE THE DELICATE FLAVOURS OF MEATLESS DISHES, AND ADDS ELEGANCE AND INTEREST TO HOME-COOKED MEALS. THE RECIPES IN THIS SECTION ARE JUST A SMALL SAMPLE OF THE ENORMOUS WORLDWIDE REPERTOIRE OF SAUCES FOR PASTA, MAIN COURSES, PASTRY DISHES AND VEGETABLES. THICKER SAUCES ARE SERVED AS DIPS FOR RAW VEGETABLES, FRUIT, BREAD AND TORTILLA CHIPS.

HOLLANDAISE

FOR 4

3 tbs white wine vinegar

2 tbs cold water

3 free-range egg yolks, beaten

6oz (175g) margarine, warmed

fresh lemon juice to taste

sea salt and freshly ground black pepper

An elegant sauce for steamed vegetables through the seasons, either hot or cold. It is also delicious with crudités as a starter. If you like, stir in a little Greek yogurt or crème fraîche.

METHOD: Boil the vinegar and water hard until reduced to 1 tbs. Put into a bowl and place it over gently heating water in a saucepan. Add the egg yolks and stir thoroughly, then gradually stir in little portions of the margarine. Stir constantly. If the sauce thickens too quickly add a few drops of cold water. Do not overheat. Season to taste with lemon juice, salt and pepper.

LEFT TO RIGHT: Hollandaise, Simple Pesto, Rich Tomato and Light Tomato Sauces.

BÉCHAMEL SAUCE

MAKES ¾ pint (450 ml)

2 oz (50g) butter or margarine

3 tbs plain flour

¾ pint (450ml) skimmed or soya milk, warmed

pinch of grated nutmeg

sea salt and freshly ground pepper

METHOD: Melt the butter in a small, heavy-bottomed saucepan. Gradually stir in the flour, using a wooden spoon. Add the warm milk slowly, stirring all the time until the sauce thickens. Season to taste with nutmeg, salt and pepper and simmer over a very low heat for 5–6 minutes.

For ½ pint (300 ml) béchamel, use 1½ oz (40g) butter or margarine, 2 tbs plain flour and ½ pint (300 ml) milk.

LIGHT TOMATO SAUCE ♥

FOR 2-3

1 x 14oz (400g) can tomatoes, or same weight fresh tomatoes, skinned (see page 36) and chopped

2 shallots or 4 spring onions, chopped finely

1 tbs dried mixed herbs

1 large clove garlic, crushed

sea salt and freshly ground black pepper

The simplest possible way of making tomato sauce, and beautifully healthy. Use plum tomatoes when they are in season; at other times of the year, make the sauce with canned tomatoes.

METHOD: Put all the ingredients into the blender and blend until smooth. Season to taste. Heat through gently for 5–6 minutes before serving.

RICH TOMATO SAUCE ♥

FOR 6

3½ lb (1.5 kg) ripe tomatoes, skinned (see page 36), or 2 x 1½ lb (700g) cans tomatoes, drained

2 tbs olive oil

1 large onion, chopped

2 tbs chopped garlic

6oz (175g) tomato purée

1 tbs chopped fresh oregano or tarragon

1 tbs each chopped fresh basil and thyme

sea salt and freshly ground pepper

This goes really well with pasta, or with anything grilled on the barbecue.

METHOD: Cut fresh or canned tomatoes into small cubes. Heat the olive oil and sauté the onion and garlic, stirring, for 1 minute. Add the chopped tomatoes and the tomato purée, then the herbs. Stir well and bring to a simmer. Cook over a very low heat, covered, for 20–25 minutes. Season to taste.

ROASTED RED PEPPER SAUCE

MAKES ½ pint (300 ml)

2 large red peppers

½ pint (300ml) vegetable stock

1oz (25g) margarine

2 tbs flour

2-3 tbs crème fraîche or single cream

This sauce needs no seasoning – it has an absolutely amazing flavour, which comes from roasting the peppers, and the most beautiful colour.

METHOD: Cut the peppers in half and deseed them. Place on a baking tray and roast at 200°C/400°F/gas 6 for 15–20 minutes, then cool. Skin them, chop roughly and blend with the stock to a thin purée.

Heat the margarine, stir in the flour and gradually stir in the purée with a wooden spoon. When it is thickened and smooth, simmer gently for 3–4 minutes. Remove from the heat, stir in the crème fraîche or single cream and serve.

BARBECUE SAUCE ᵥ

MAKES 1 pint (600 ml)

12oz (350g) tomato ketchup

juice of 1 lemon

¼ pint (150ml) red or white wine vinegar

6 cloves garlic, crushed

2 heaped tbs soft brown sugar

2 tbs olive oil

2 tbs mild mustard

2 tbs sweet cucumber relish

The perfect sauce for marinating vegetables before you put them on the barbecue – sharp, and full of flavour. Hand it around to go with barbecued vegetables as well as vegetarian burgers and sausages.

METHOD: Put the tomato ketchup into a bowl with the lemon juice. Measure the vinegar and pour it into the ketchup bottle; shake well so that you clean the bottle, and add the liquid to the bowl. Mix thoroughly, then stir in the rest of the ingredients and it is ready to use. Keep refrigerated in an airtight jar.

CHILLI SAUCE v

MAKES ¾ pint (450 ml)

1 sweet onion, chopped small

1 tbs olive oil

1 large clove garlic, crushed

1-2 fresh green chillies, sliced finely

1 x 14oz (400g) can chopped tomatoes with juice, or same weight fresh tomatoes, skinned (see page 36) and chopped

juice of ½ lemon

sea salt

A full-blooded chilli sauce, rich and full of flavour. It is always welcome at a barbecue party. Try it with the quesadillas on page 21.

METHOD: Soften the onion in the olive oil over a low heat, covered with a lid, for 5–6 minutes. Add the garlic and chilli and cook for a few minutes longer, until the chilli is well softened. Add the tomatoes and heat through for 5 minutes. Finish with the lemon juice and season to taste with salt. Keep refrigerated in an airtight jar.

TOMATO AND CHILLI SALSA v

FOR 2–3

5 tomatoes, skinned (see page 36) and cubed small

juice of 1½ lemons

6oz (175g) canned mild green chillies, chopped small, or fresh chillies to taste

½ purple or red onion, chopped finely

sea salt

1 tbs chopped fresh coriander (optional)

An easy, quickly made sauce, this is lovely with barbecued foods (see pages 66–71), and with anything Mexican (see pages 20–27).

METHOD: Mix all the ingredients together and simmer for 10–15 minutes over a very gentle heat. Season to taste with a little salt and stir in the optional coriander.

CHILLI HEAT

If using fresh chillies, remove the seeds and veins first if you want to control the heat.

TARRAGON AND MUSTARD SAUCE

MAKES ½ pint (300 ml)

1 oz (25 g) margarine

4 tbs chopped fresh tarragon or 2 tbs dried tarragon

1 tbs mild mustard

1 tbs cornflour

4 fl oz (125 ml) milk

¼ pint (150 ml) crème fraîche or single cream

A fine sauce that turns the simplest of meals into something special.
Try it with the stuffed peppers on page 32.

METHOD: Melt the margarine and cook the tarragon in it very gently for 2–3 minutes. Stir in the mustard and mix well. Sprinkle in the cornflour and stir until smooth, then gradually add the milk, stirring all the time. When the sauce is smooth and thick, stir in the crème fraîche. The sauce needs no further seasoning – the tarragon flavour does it all.

ARTICHOKE DIP

FOR 4

8 oz (250 g) artichoke hearts, canned or freshly cooked

½ red onion, chopped finely

1 clove garlic, crushed

2 tbs finely chopped parsley

1 tbs chopped fresh oregano or 1 tsp dried oregano

2 oz (50 g) pecorino cheese, grated

¼ pint (150 ml) mayonnaise

sea salt and freshly ground black pepper

A delicately flavoured dip that goes very well on a mixed buffet table. Or hand it around with corn chips or raw vegetables, as a nibble before a meal.

METHOD: Put all the ingredients into the blender and blend until smooth. Season to taste and chill. Serve with corn chips, sliced carrots or celery.

DEALING WITH ONIONS

Peeling pungent onions can make your eyes water, so rinse your hands frequently – it will reduce the effect of the onions.

Softening onions in oil or margarine, which is such a basic step in so many recipes, is best done by first tossing the sliced or chopped onions in the oil or fat over a moderate heat until well coated and then turning the heat down very low, covering the pan with a lid and leaving the onions to cook very gently for 10–12 minutes. They become very soft and sweet because this process steams them rather than browns them. Stir just once or twice during the cooking.

Browning onions is done over a higher heat – and they taste much stronger than onions softened by the method above.

AMERICAN SOURED CREAM DIP

FOR 4–6

1 packet dried onion soup mix
(approx 2 oz/50g)

¾ pint (450 ml) soured cream

Simplicity itself, this dip is amazingly
delicious and a huge favourite. Serve with tortilla
chips, crisps and a selection of crudités.

METHOD: Stir the dried soup mix into the soured cream
and put into a decorative bowl. Chill for 1 hour or so before
serving to allow the flavours to blend.

SIMPLE PESTO SAUCE v

MAKES 2 fl oz (60 ml)

8-10 large cloves garlic,
crushed or chopped

2 large bunches fresh basil,
chopped

4 tbs olive oil

Serve with pasta for a quick, delicious meal.

METHOD: Combine the ingredients in a bowl and mix
together. Chill before using.

For traditional pesto, add 4 tbs pine nuts and 3 oz (75 g)
freshly grated Parmesan cheese. Pound together in a mortar
and pestle, or blend until creamy in a blender or food
processor. Store in an airtight jar in the refrigerator.

GUACAMOLE v

FOR 4–6

2 tomatoes, skinned (see page
36) and chopped

juice of 2 large lemons

1 small fresh red chilli, sliced
very finely

2 cloves garlic, sliced finely

4 spring onions, sliced finely

2 large avocados, mashed

sea salt and freshly ground
black pepper

There are endless versions of this famous
Mexican avocado dip: here is mine! Serve with tortilla
chips, pitta bread, or raw mushrooms,
celery, carrots and other crudités of your choice.

METHOD: Combine all the ingredients except the avocado in
the food processor and work until very smooth. (Substitute
one 4 oz (125g) can of mild green chillies, chopped finely, if
you find fresh chillies too hot.) Stir in the avocado with a
fork and season to taste. Put into a decorative bowl.

GREEN HERB MAYONNAISE

MAKES ½ pint (300 ml)

2 tbs chopped fresh tarragon or dill

2 tbs each chopped parsley, chives and watercress

2 tbs chopped baby spinach leaves

½ pint (300 ml) mayonnaise

METHOD: Chop the fresh herbs and leaves finely in a food processor. Add them to the mayonnaise and stir in thoroughly until well blended.

THE FOOD PROCESSOR

If you haven't already got one, a food processor is the best investment you can make as a keen cook. It does so many things, and much faster than you can do them yourself. It makes wonderful smooth soups; it shreds vegetables in an instant; it makes vegetable purées without effort; it grates, slices and chops very very finely; it makes breadcrumbs and pastry dough; and it will produce worry-free mayonnaise and other emulsion sauces.

DILL CUCUMBER DIP

FOR 4

½ cucumber, grated

½ pint (300 ml) soured cream

4 tbs chopped fresh dill

2 tbs dried dillweed

1 tbs finely chopped onion

juice of ½ lemon

sea salt and freshly ground black pepper

This pale green dip has a lovely summery flavour, and makes light food for hot weather.
Serve with crisps, raw vegetables or granary toast, or as a sauce for a main dish.

METHOD: Squeeze the grated cucumber dry then pat on kitchen paper. Put all the ingredients into a bowl and mix thoroughly. Put into a dish and chill for at least 1 hour before serving.

DESSERTS AND CAKES

VERY FEW PEOPLE CAN RESIST A REALLY DELICIOUS DESSERT OR SLICE OF CAKE, AND
JUDICIOUS AMOUNTS OF SOMETHING SWEET AT REGULAR INTERVALS ARE NOT SUCH A BAD
THING FOR GENERAL HEALTH. FRUIT DESSERTS ARE WELL-LOVED, AND FRUIT SALADS AND
SORBETS MAKE GOOD USE OF FRAGRANT SOFT FRUITS IN SUMMER. CLASSIC CAKES ARE
ALSO ONE OF THE PLEASURES OF HOME COOKING AND FAMILY LIFE.

RASPBERRY MOUSSE

FOR 4

*3 oz (85 g) vegetarian
raspberry jelly crystals*

1 pint (600 ml) water

*½ pint (300 ml) whipping
cream*

*8 oz (250 g) fresh or thawed
frozen raspberries*

*whipped cream and chopped
nuts to decorate*

This basic fruit mousse can be endlessly varied,
using other fruits (in season or frozen)
with their matching jelly or a contrasting flavour.
Vegetarian jellies use agar agar, made from
seaweed, as the setting agent, rather than gelatine
(which is derived from animals).

METHOD: Make the jelly with the water as directed on
the packet. Leave it to cool but not set.

Whip the cream. Whip the jelly and fold in the whipped
cream. Fold in the fruit. Pour into a dish or mould and chill
until set.

Serve in the dish, or turned out of the mould, decorated
with whipped cream and chopped nuts.

Since vegetarian jelly sets less hard than regular jelly,
some separation may occur. If this happens, mix the mousse
up again and serve in the dish, decorated as above.

REDCURRANT CHEESECAKE

FOR 6-8

6oz (175g) digestive biscuits

2oz (50g) margarine, melted

2lb (1kg) low fat soft cheese

6oz (175g) light soft brown sugar

½ pint (300ml) double cream, whipped

8oz (250g) redcurrants, topped and tailed

A very easy uncooked cheesecake, with redcurrants folded into cheese and cream, on a crunchy biscuit base.

METHOD: Crumble the biscuits finely (you can use a food processor for this if you have one). Add the melted margarine and mix thoroughly. Press evenly over the bottom of a greased 8 inch (20 cm) loose-bottomed flan tin. Chill until set.

Beat the soft cheese with the sugar until creamy. Fold in the whipped cream, then carefully fold in the redcurrants. Pile on to the prepared base and smooth the surface. Chill for several hours, or overnight, before serving.

PECAN PIE

FOR 6

6oz (175g) sweetcrust pastry (see page 104)

2oz (50g) margarine

4oz (125g) light soft brown sugar

2 free-range eggs, beaten

1 tbs plain flour

¼ pint (150ml) golden syrup

5 tbs skimmed milk

1 tsp vanilla essence

6oz (175g) shelled pecan nuts

A great American classic, this recipe brings out the best in the delicious pecan nut. Serve warm or at room temperature, with thick cream.

METHOD: Roll out the pastry dough and line an 8 inch (20 cm) loose-bottomed flan tin. Bake blind until part cooked (see page 61).

Cream the margarine with the sugar until light and fluffy, then beat in the eggs. Beat in the flour, syrup and milk. Add the vanilla and beat thoroughly until the mixture is light.

Sprinkle the nuts over the bottom of the pastry case and pour the mixture over them. Bake at 190°C/375°F/gas 5 for 15 minutes, then turn the heat down to 170°C/325°F/gas 3 and continue baking for 30 minutes or until a knife inserted in the centre comes out clean.

CHOCOLATE DELIGHT

FOR 8–10

½ pint (300ml) milk

a dash of sherry

8oz (250g) trifle sponges, split in half horizontally

6oz (175g) margarine

4oz (125g) caster sugar

pinch of salt

6 free-range eggs, separated

8oz (250g) plain chocolate

½ pint (300ml) double cream, whipped

grated plain chocolate to decorate

This sumptuous dessert of sherry-moistened sponge surrounding a rich chocolate mousse filling, all covered with whipped cream, is always a huge success. Everyone asks for the recipe, so here it is!

METHOD: Mix the milk with the sherry in a shallow dish. Dip the split trifle sponges in it briefly to moisten, then use to line a greased 8 inch (20 cm) soufflé dish. Line the sides first and then cover the bottom.

Cream the margarine with the sugar and salt until light and fluffy, then beat in the egg yolks. Beat until the mixture is pale yellow. Melt the chocolate in a bowl over hot water, or in the microwave. Gradually beat the chocolate into the egg yolk mixture. In another bowl, whisk the egg whites until very stiff and fold into the mixture. Pour into the sponge-lined dish, cover and chill for at least 24 hours.

Turn out, cover with whipped cream and decorate with grated chocolate.

OVERLEAF: (left to right) Crème Brûlée, Redcurrant Cheesecake, Chocolate Delight and Pecan Pie

CRÈME BRÛLÉE

FOR 6

1¼ lb (625 g) crème fraîche

thinly pared rind of 1 lemon, cut into thin strips

4 egg yolks from size-1 free-range eggs

3 tbs caster sugar

a few drops of vanilla essence

6 tbs light soft brown sugar

This is a healthier version of a famous classic, using crème fraîche instead of double cream. To vary the dessert, put halved seeded grapes, redcurrants, sliced banana or pear in the bottom of each ramekin before pouring in the custard.

METHOD: Simmer the crème fraîche with the lemon rind gently for 10 minutes. Leave to cool for 10 minutes. Beat the egg yolks with the caster sugar in a heat-proof bowl until pale and creamy, add the vanilla essence and then strain in the crème fraîche, stirring well. Place the bowl over a pan of hot – not boiling – water and cook for 20–25 minutes or until the custard thickens, stirring occasionally. Don't let the water come to boiling point at any stage. When ready, the custard will be velvety in consistency and will lightly coat the back of a spoon. Put into 6 ramekin dishes and chill overnight.

The next day, sprinkle 1 tbs light brown sugar over the top of each custard and smooth evenly. Place under a very hot grill for 3–4 minutes or until the sugar has melted and is bubbling. Leave to cool, then chill again for up to 8 hours.

FRUIT SORBET v

FOR 6

*1½ lb (750g) fresh or frozen
raspberries, strawberries or
other fruit of your choice*

about 4oz (125g) sugar

4 tbs water

juice of 1 lemon

A refreshing fruit sorbet is the perfect
dessert in hot weather. You can make it sweet or
a little tart, according to your taste.

METHOD: Purée the fruit in a blender or food processor.
If it has small pips (as raspberries do), press the purée
through a sieve.

Combine the sugar and water in a saucepan and heat,
stirring to dissolve the sugar. Bring to the boil and boil the
syrup until it reaches 113°C/230°F on a sugar thermometer.
Remove from the heat and leave to cool.

When the syrup is cold, mix it with the fruit purée and
stir in the lemon juice. Taste and add more sugar or lemon
juice if liked: the flavour should be quite strong.

Pour into an ice-cream machine and freeze until firm.

TIRAMISÙ

FOR 4–6

*¼ pint (150ml) strong black
coffee*

2 tbs brandy

*6oz (175g) sponge fingers
(boudoir biscuits)*

*8oz (250g) mascarpone or
full fat soft cheese*

4 oz (125g) plain yogurt

4 oz (125g) ricotta cheese

4 oz (125g) caster sugar

1 tsp vanilla essence

3 free-range egg whites

1 tbs grated chocolate

This is an absolutely brilliant version of a world-
famous dessert – slightly less rich than
some recipes, but full of that coffee flavour, and
well laced with brandy!

METHOD: Mix the coffee with the brandy in a shallow
dish. Dip half of the sponge fingers very briefly into the
mixture to moisten them, then use to line the bottom of a
glass bowl. Mix together the mascarpone, yogurt and ricotta
until smooth, and add the sugar and vanilla. Whisk the egg
whites until stiff and fold into the cheese mixture. Spoon
half of this over the layer of sponge fingers. Make a second
layer of moistened sponge fingers and cover with the rest of
the cheese mixture. Sprinkle grated chocolate on top, cover
and chill for several hours before serving.

FROZEN VANILLA MOUSSE

FOR 3–4

8 fl oz (250ml) whipping cream

1 oz (25g) icing sugar, sifted

½ tsp vanilla essence

1 free-range egg white

¼ tsp salt

This mousse is like a simple ice cream made without a custard. The mousse can also be made with Greek yogurt, rather than cream, and weetened with honey instead of sugar. You can stir a little stewed fresh or dried fruit or chopped nuts into the cream mixture before folding in the egg white, to vary the flavour.

METHOD: Whip the cream until it is starting to thicken. Add the icing sugar and vanilla and continue whipping until the cream is thick.

In another bowl, whisk the egg white with the salt until stiff. Fold the egg white into the cream mixture. Spoon into a mould or ice cube tray, cover and freeze without stirring. Serve with a sauce or with crushed soft fruits.

FLOATING ISLANDS

FOR 6–8

1¾ pints (1 litre) milk

3 free-range eggs, separated

4 oz (125g) caster sugar

1 tbs cornflour

½ tsp salt

½ tsp vanilla or almond essence, or ¼ tsp ground mixed spice

seedless raspberry jam

No one can resist this pudding of tender poached meringue 'islands' floating on a custard 'sea'. The custard is stabilized with cornflour, which will prevent any curdling.

METHOD: Heat the milk in a wide saucepan. Meanwhile, put 2 of the egg whites in a bowl and whisk until frothy. Add 2 tbs of the sugar and whisk until stiff.

Drop large heaping spoonfuls of the egg whites on to the hot milk, to make 6 or 8 meringues. Poach gently until the meringues feel just firm to the touch, turning them over so that they are cooked on both sides, about 2 minutes each side. When they are ready, remove with a slotted spoon and drain on paper towels. Reserve the hot milk.

Combine the remaining sugar, cornflour and salt in a bowl and stir to mix. Add the remaining egg white and the egg yolks and mix together until smoothly blended. Pour in the hot milk, stirring. Pour the custard mixture into the top of a double boiler set over simmering water, or into a heavy-based saucepan, and cook until thickened, stirring constantly. Remove from the heat and cool slightly, then stir in the essence or spice. Pour the custard into a wide serving dish and leave to cool completely. Before serving, arrange the meringues on top of the custard and dot with raspberry jam.

VEGAN FRUIT CAKE ♥

MAKES a 9½ x 6 inch (24 x 15 cm) cake

12oz (320g) sultanas

9oz (280g) currants

14oz (400g) glacé cherries, halved

5oz (150g) raisins, chopped

2 tbs chopped glacé ginger (optional)

4 tbs golden syrup

3½oz (90g) margarine

16fl oz (500ml) unsweetened orange juice

8fl oz (250ml) soya milk

8oz (250g) wholemeal plain flour

8oz (250g) wholemeal self-raising flour

2 tsp ground mixed spice

This rich, dark, moist cake contains no sugar, just a little golden syrup, relying instead on the natural sweetness of the dried fruits and fruit juice. Wrapped tightly and stored in an airtight tin, the cake will keep very well.

METHOD: Combine the fruits, ginger, golden syrup, margarine and fruit juice in a large saucepan. Stir over a low heat until the margarine has melted, then cover the pan and simmer for 5 minutes. Pour the fruit mixture into a large bowl and leave to cool to room temperature.

Add the soya milk and stir to mix. Sift the flours and spice into the bowl (tip in the bran left in the sieve) and mix thoroughly.

Pour the cake mixture into a greased 9½ x 6 inch (24 x 15 cm) rectangular cake tin lined with 3 layers of greaseproof paper, and bake at 170°C/325°F/gas 3 for about 1½ hours or until a skewer inserted into the centre comes out clean. Leave to cool, in the tin, on a wire rack.

CARROT CAKE WITH CREAM CHEESE FROSTING

FOR 10–12

8oz (250g) plain flour

8oz (250g) light soft brown sugar

pinch of salt

1 tsp baking powder

2 tsp ground cinnamon

6fl oz (175ml) sunflower oil

2 free-range eggs, lightly beaten

1 tsp vanilla essence

1lb (500g) cooked carrots, puréed

4oz (125g) walnuts, chopped

2oz (50g) desiccated coconut

For the cream cheese frosting:

8oz (250g) low fat soft cheese

8oz (250g) icing sugar

1 tbs fresh lemon juice

This rich carrot cake is made with cooked puréed carrots, which makes it deliciously moist, and it has some coconut and walnuts in it as well to add texture. Wonderful at teatime, and also as a dessert.

METHOD: Sift the dry ingredients into a bowl. Add the oil, eggs and vanilla and beat well. The mixture will be quite sticky. Beat in the carrots, mixing thoroughly. Fold in the walnuts and coconut.

Pour into a greased 8 inch (20 cm) cake tin and bake at 180°C/350°F/gas 4 for 1¼ hours or until a sharp knife inserted into the centre comes out clean. Cool on a rack.

To make the cream cheese frosting, mash the cheese and slowly sift in the icing sugar, beating until fully incorporated. Stir in the lemon juice.

When the cake is cold, cut it in half horizontally and fill with one-third of the cream cheese frosting. Spread the remaining frosting over the top and sides of the cake.

AUSTRIAN SHORTCRUST PASTRY

MAKES 1 lb (500 g)

5 oz (150g) margarine

5 oz (150g) plain flour

3 oz (75g) caster sugar

3 oz (75g) ground almonds

1 free-range egg yolk

1 tsp grated lemon rind

METHOD: Rub the margarine lightly into the sifted flour until the mixture resembles fine breadcrumbs. Stir in the sugar and ground almonds. Mix in the egg yolk and lemon rind and knead on a lightly floured board until smooth. Chill for 30 minutes. When ready to cook, roll out to ¼ inch (6 mm) thickness on a floured board.

SWEETCRUST PASTRY ♥

MAKES 12 oz (350 g)

8 oz (250g) plain flour

1 tbs caster sugar

4 oz (125g) margarine

3 tbs cold water

METHOD: Sift the flour into a large bowl and stir in the sugar. Rub in the margarine lightly until the mixture resembles fine breadcrumbs. Bind with the water. Knead lightly on a floured board until smooth. Wrap and chill for at least 30 minutes before rolling out.

The Vegetarian Pantry

Basic Processed Foods

- canned tomatoes
- canned sweetcorn
- canned beans: cannellini, butter, red kidney, borlotti, flageolet etc
- canned baked beans
- pasta: wholemeal and plain
- wholemeal bread
- soya products: soya milk, tofu, tempeh, vegetarian mince, vegetarian steak chunks, soy sauce, tamari
- vegetable stock cubes
- vegetarian gravy mix
- Marmite, yeast extract
- curry powder
- tomato purée
- tomato ketchup, pickles, relishes, chutneys, mustards
- mayonnaise
- Oriental sauces: black bean, garlic, yellow bean, etc
- Mexican taco sauces and relishes

Frozen Products

- there is now a wide range of readymade frozen vegetarian meals available from supermarkets, including my own brand. These convenient products are ideal for busy cooks

Dairy Products

- free-range eggs
- vegetarian cheese
- plain yogurt

Spreads, Oils and Vinegars

- polyunsaturated margarine (read the label for hidden animal products)
- tahini
- vegetable pastes
- vinegars: cider, wine, rice, balsamic
- olive oil
- vegetable oils: sunflower, grapeseed, soya, groundnut
- dark sesame oil
- walnut oil
- honey, jams (low sugar and homemade), maple syrup

Cereals

- barley, buckwheat, cornmeal, millet, oats, wheat
- rice
- wild rice
- unbleached organic flour

Dried Fruit

- raisins, sultanas, currants
- apples
- apricots
- glacé cherries
- mixed peel
- peaches
- pears
- prunes

Dried Pulses

- dried beans: black, black-eye, borlotti, butter, haricot, flageolet, mung, red kidney, soya
- lentils: red, green, brown
- split peas
- chick peas

Basic Plant Foods

- nuts: almonds, brazils, cashews, hazelnuts, peanuts, pecans, pine kernels, pistachios, walnuts
- seeds: pumpkin, sesame, sunflower, poppy
- dried coconut
- capers
- olives
- sun-dried tomatoes
- chillies: dried and in brine

Herbs and Spices

- sea salt, peppercorns
- vanilla: pods, extract
- herbal teas
- the complete range: fresh and dried herbs, whole and ground spices, to your taste

Fruit and Vegetables

- plenty of fresh, organic fruit and vegetables in season

PULSES

Pulses, which include beans, peas and lentils, are very versatile, and they are an excellent source of protein, carbohydrate, vitamins and minerals, as well as being low in fat and high in fibre. The soya bean is the best source of quality protein.

Dried pulses need to be soaked overnight, in plenty of water to cover, before cooking. The exceptions are lentils and split peas: large whole lentils and large split peas need only 2–3 hours soaking, and very small red lentils and small split peas need no soaking at all.

To cook pulses, drain off the soaking water and rinse them, then put into a saucepan and cover with fresh water. (If cooking red kidney beans, bring to the boil, boil for 10 minutes, then drain and put back in the pan with fresh cold water to cover.) Add a bay leaf and a slice or two of onion for extra flavour. Bring to the boil and simmer, covered, for the time given in the chart below. Wait to add salt until 10 minutes before the end of the cooking time – it toughens the skins and hardens them if you add it earlier.

Dried pulses double their weight after being soaked and cooked, so when using them instead of canned pulses in a recipe, use half the weight of the canned pulses given. In other words, for 8 oz (250 g) canned kidney beans, soak and cook 4 oz (125 g) dried kidney beans.

When using canned pulses in a recipe, it's best to add them towards the end of the cooking time so that they don't go mushy. Drain them well and rinse them under running cold water before you use them.

COOKING TIMES FOR PULSES, AFTER SOAKING

Aduki beans . . . . 30–60 minutes
Black-eye beans . . . . 1½ hours
Borlotti beans . . . . 1 hour
Butter beans . . . . 1–1½ hours
Cannellini beans . . . . 1 hour
Chick peas . . . . 1½–2 hours
Flageolets. . . . . 45 minutes
Haricot beans . . . . 1–1½ hours
Lentils, large brown or green . . . . 45 minutes
Mung beans . . . . 40 minutes
Red kidney beans. . . . . 1–1½ hours
Soya beans . . . . 3–4 hours
Split peas, large . . . . 40–50 minutes

COOKING TIMES FOR PULSES WHICH REQUIRE
NO PRE-SOAKING

Lentils, small red. . . . . 20–30 minutes
Split peas, small. . . . . 45–60 minutes

SOYA PRODUCTS

The soya bean is the seed of the soya bean plant. It has been used as a staple in the Chinese diet for more than 4,000 years. From the soya bean come many soya products that are widely used in a vegetarian diet. These include:

• soya milk, which is made by soaking soya beans in water and then straining. Soya cheese and soya yogurt are made from soya milk.

• tofu, which is a curd made from coagulated soya milk. (Vegans can use tofu in place of yogurt in soups, dips, salad dressings and sauces. 'Silken' tofu, which is widely available, is light and creamy and works very well in all these recipes.)

• tempeh, which is a fermented soya bean paste made by mixing cooked soya beans with a fungus that holds it together.

• miso, which is a fermented condiment made from soya beans, grain (rice or barley), salt and water.

• soya or soy sauce (shoyu), which is made by fermenting soya beans with cracked roasted wheat, salt and water.

• tamari, another soy sauce, similar to shoyu but slightly stronger and made without wheat.

• soya margarine and soya oil, both of which are high in polyunsaturated fats and low in saturated fats

• soya flour

• TVP, or textured vegetable protein, which is de-fatted soya flour, processed and dried to provide a substance that has a spongy texture, similar to meat. A good source of fibre and high quality protein, TVP is also fortified with vitamin B12.

WHEAT

Wheat protein, which is derived from wheat gluten, can be processed to resemble closely the texture of meat and is widely used as a meat substitute.

COOKING WITH MEAT SUBSTITUTES

Meat substitutes are available as mince and chunks, as well as sausages and burgers. All can be found in supermarkets and health food stores. The joy of using vegetarian mince and chunks is that you can take them straight from the freezer – there's no need to thaw them. Just measure out the amount called for in the recipe and add it as directed. You can use them in curries, for spaghetti or lasagne – any dish where you would expect to find mince or stewing steak. (Readers in Great Britain can also find mince and chunks in chilled form – use them exactly as you would the frozen version.)

To brown vegetarian mince or steak chunks (which brings out their flavour), sauté them lightly in 2 tbs hot oil for each 8 oz (250 g). If you are in a hurry you can use these products without browning them first, although they will be slightly less tasty.

As a general rule, every 1 lb (500 g) mince or chunks needs at least ¾ pint (450 ml) liquid in their sauce since they are usually more absorbent than meat. Neither vegetarian mince nor chunks need much salt, so season judiciously.

VEGETARIAN CHEESE

To make cheese, a substance called rennet is used to coagulate milk, separating it into curds and whey. The curds are treated to make cheese, and the liquid whey finds its way into margarines and many other products. Vegetarian cheese is made with rennets of non-animal origin.

Fig leaves, thistle, melon and safflower have provided the country housewife with plant rennets in the past, but today most vegetarian cheeses are made using rennet produced by a fungus, Mucor miehei, or from a bacteria (Bacillus subtilis). Animal rennet, which contains the enzyme chymosin, is usually obtained from the stomach of newly born calves. Advances in genetic engineering have led to the synthesizing of chymosin, which may soon replace animal rennet.

Vegetarian cheeses are usually clearly labelled. Vegetarian versions of cream cheese and other soft cheeses, Cheddar, Cheshire, double Gloucester, stilton, brie, dolcelatte and other blue cheeses, feta and ricotta can all be found in major supermarkets. Cottage cheese is always vegetarian. Parmesan is normally made with animal rennet, although a vegetarian version is emerging. Mozzarella is not always vegetarian.

Cheese is a good source of protein, as well as calcium, zinc, vitamin B12 and a little iron. New vegetarians should be wary of eating too much cheese as it contains a lot of saturated fat and can lead to high cholesterol levels.

MUSHROOMS

In some parts of the world gathering wild mushrooms is a national pastime, a family outing to harvest the ceps, chanterelles, boletus, parasol and field mushrooms that grow in the woods and fields at certain times of the year. Gathering mushrooms is a wonderful experience, akin to a treasure hunt, and you are well rewarded when you deliver them to the table.

Obviously you have to be careful not to pick the wrong ones, but the poisonous mushrooms are easily identifiable with a good field guide. So take to the woods and fields and enjoy the pleasures of both the hunt and the table.

NUTRITION FOR VEGETARIANS

A good diet is a balanced diet: it is the overall mixture that counts. The important thing is to eat a wide variety of foods to give you the nutrients that the body needs to maintain growth, to repair itself, to provide energy, and to resist infection. At least once a day, everyone should eat a well-balanced meal, which means one that contains sufficient carbohydrate, protein, fat, dietary fibre, water, vitamins and minerals for individual needs. These dietary needs vary according to sex, age, activity levels, physical condition and climate. These guidelines should help ensure that you are getting a good nutritional balance in your diet.

ENERGY AND WATER

Food is the fuel that gives the human body energy, thus enabling it to work. The right amount of food is essential for normal biological processes such as breathing and pumping blood round the body, to perform muscular work and to maintain body temperature. Certain foods provide more energy than others; some provide it quickly while others release it slowly into the system.

Water comprises two-thirds of our body weight, and we cannot survive for more than a few days without water. Many foods contain high levels, but it is also important to drink sufficient water on a daily basis: experts suggest 1¾–3½ pints (1–2 litres) every day.

PROTEIN

Proteins are made up from various combinations of amino acids that are required by our bodies for growth and repair. Both plant proteins and animal proteins contain these amino acids, so it is a fallacy that we can only get protein from an animal source. Excess amounts of protein cannot be stored in the body, so eating more than you need can have no benefit. In fact, it can be harmful – many western meat-eating diets contain far too much protein and this is now thought to cause diseases including certain cancers and osteoporosis, as well as poor kidney function.

A healthy, balanced diet containing a variety of foods will provide all the protein you require.

GOOD SOURCES OF PROTEIN Pulses, soya products (tofu, soya milk, etc), nuts, seeds, rice, pasta, wheat flour, bread, muesli, oatmeal, cheese, eggs, milk, yogurt, potatoes, peas, cauliflower, broccoli, garlic, sweetcorn.

CARBOHYDRATE

Carbohydrate is a major source of energy in the diet, and most of it is provided by plant foods. There are three main types of carbohydrate in food: sugars, starches and cellulose. Cellulose is the indigestible part of plant foods and is the main constituent of dietary fibre. This stimulates the digestive system, helps prevent constipation and reduces the risk of colon cancer and disease.

GOOD SOURCES OF CARBOHYDRATE Pulses, rice, pasta, buckwheat groats, bulgar wheat, oatmeal, bread, nuts, potatoes, root vegetables, peas, sweetcorn, onions, garlic, dried apricots, bananas, mangoes.

GOOD SOURCES OF DIETARY FIBRE Pulses, nuts, wholemeal bread, wholemeal pasta, wheat bran, oats and other whole grains, most vegetables, raspberries, blackberries, redcurrants, dates, figs, prunes, dried apricots.

FAT AND CHOLESTEROL

Fat provides energy in a more concentrated form than carbohydrate and converts very easily into body fat. Although a certain amount of fat is necessary to provide warmth and essential nutrients and to protect the internal organs, the average western diet contains too much. Fats from animal sources contain a high proportion of saturated fatty acids, which raise blood cholesterol levels and increase the risk of heart disease.

Cholesterol is unique to animals and humans. It is made mainly in the liver and is present in all of the body's tissues. We need cholesterol but we do not necessarily need it in the diet: for some people an excess can cause health problems. This is why people on a diet containing no animal products are thought to be less at risk from heart disease.

SOURCES OF FAT Cheese, cream, yogurt, whole milk, butter, margarine, egg yolk, nuts, seeds, avocados, olives, vegetable oils, oats.

VITAMINS

Small amounts of vitamins are essential for the regulation of all bodily processes. With the exception of vitamin D, the body cannot make its own vitamins, and some cannot be stored. Vitamins must therefore be obtained from food on a daily basis. A vegetarian diet can provide all the necessary vitamins.

VITAMIN A

Required for healthy skin and mucus membranes, and for night vision. Thought to help prevent the development of cancer.

GOOD SOURCES OF VITAMIN A Butter, margarine, milk, cheese, yogurt, cream, sweet potatoes, butternut squash, carrots, red peppers, chillies, leeks, lettuce, broccoli, Swiss chard, spinach, tomatoes, watercress, basil, coriander, parsley, apricots, canteloupe melons, mangoes.

B VITAMINS

A group of eight actual vitamins and several vitamin-like compounds. The main ones include:
Thiamin (B1): Releases energy from carbohydrate, alcohol and fat.
Riboflavin (B2): Releases energy from protein, fat and carbohydrate.
Niacin (B3): Involved in the oxidative release of energy from food; protects the skin and helps improve circulation.
Vitamin B6: Essential for protein metabolism, and for the formation of haemoglobin.
Vitamin B12: Helps protect nerves and is involved in the formation of red blood cells.
Folate: Involved in the formation of new cells and therefore essential for the normal growth and development of the foetus.

GOOD SOURCES OF B VITAMINS Eggs, cheese, milk, pulses, wholemeal bread, brown rice, fortified breakfast cereals, nuts, seeds, yeast extract, avocados, cauliflower, cabbage, peas, potatoes, mushrooms, green leafy vegetables, dates, figs, currants, dried apricots, clementines, canteloupe melon.

VITAMIN C

Essential for the formation of bones, teeth and tissues. Speeds the healing of wounds, helps maintain elasticity of the skin, aids the absorption of iron and improves resistance to infection. May help prevent the occurrence and development of cancer.

GOOD SOURCES OF VITAMIN C Broccoli, Brussels sprouts, cauliflower, cabbage, mangetout, green leafy vegetables, red peppers, chillies, watercress, parsley, blackcurrants, strawberries, kiwi fruit, guavas, citrus fruit.

NOTE: With the exception of niacin (B3), these vitamins are easily destroyed by heat. Vitamin C is easily destroyed by exposure to air, and all are unstable in alkaline conditions and are water-soluble. So to maximize the intake of these vitamins, food sources should be prepared, cooked and served quickly. Steaming vegetables minimizes vitamin loss.

VITAMIN D

Needed for the absorption of calcium and the regulation of calcium levels in the blood. Sunlight activates the metabolism of vitamin D in the body.

GOOD SOURCES OF VITAMIN D Butter, margarine, cheese, cream, yogurt, milk, eggs, sunlight.

VITAMIN E

An anti-oxidant that protects the cells from attack by reactive forms of oxygen and free radicals. Involved in red blood cell formation.

GOOD SOURCES OF VITAMIN E Vegetable oils, nuts and nut oils, seeds, egg, margarine, hard cheeses, chickpeas, soya beans and soya products, wheat germ, oatmeal, avocados, olives, carrots, parsnips, red peppers, green leafy vegetables, sweet potatoes, tomatoes, sweetcorn, watercress.

VITAMIN K

Needed for effective blood clotting. A deficiency is rare due to bacterial synthesis within the body. Vitamin K is found in most vegetables.

MINERALS

Minerals perform a variety of important functions in the human body. A balanced intake is important for long-term good health. Excess of any mineral can be as dangerous as too little.

CALCIUM

Calcium is the most abundant mineral in the body, and is needed for building strong bones and teeth, for muscle contraction and blood clotting. Healthy bones are not only reliant on a good calcium intake but on regular exercise and vitamin D, which aids calcium absorption.

It should also be noted, however, that too much calcium can also be harmful as the excess is deposited in internal organs such as kidneys. This can cause serious problems and even be fatal.

Dairy foods have traditionally been thought of as the principal source of calcium, but have you ever stopped to think where the cow gets its calcium from – certainly not from dairy products!

GOOD SOURCES OF CALCIUM Milk, cheese, yogurt, sesame seeds, tofu, bread, nuts, pulses, okra, broccoli, watercress, onions, green leafy vegetables, sea vegetables, dried fruit such as raisins, apricots, pears and peaches, rhubarb, lemons, oranges, hard water.

MAGNESIUM

Needed for strong bones, and for the functioning of some of the enzymes involved in energy utilization.

GOOD SOURCES OF MAGNESIUM Cream, yogurt, cheese, eggs, bread, papadums, wheat bran, bulgar wheat, oatmeal, soya flour, wholemeal flour, brown rice, wholemeal pasta, nuts, seeds, pulses, green leafy vegetables, sea vegetables, dried fruit such as apricots, pears and peaches.

IRON

Essential component of haemoglobin, the red pigment in blood which transports oxygen though the body. Iron also assists in the production of red blood corpuscles, the metabolism of B vitamins and the functioning of several enzymes. Iron deficiency, which causes anaemia, is the most prevalent nutritional problem worldwide. It has been shown that vegetarians are no more likely to suffer from it than non-vegetarians. A good intake of vitamin C enhances absorption of iron.

GOOD SOURCES OF IRON Eggs, pulses, wholemeal bread, wheat bran, papadums, cashew nuts, pine nuts, pumpkin seeds, cumin seeds, sesame seeds, green leafy vegetables, watercress, sea vegetables, basil, mint, parsley, blackcurrants, dried fruits such as raisins, prunes, figs and peaches, cocoa.

ZINC

Present in every part of the body and vital for the healthy working of many of its functions, including a major role in enzyme reactions, the immune system and resistance to infection. It plays a crucial role in growth and cell division, in insulin activity and liver function. Men need more zinc than women because semen contains 100 times more zinc than is found in the blood, and so the more sexually active a man is, the more zinc he will require.

GOOD SOURCES OF ZINC Cheese, egg yolk, pulses, wholemeal bread, wheat bran, soya flour, yeast, nuts, pumpkin seeds, sesame seeds, tahini paste, green vegetables, garlic.

POTASSIUM

Important in maintaining the body's correct balance of fluids, required for nerve and muscle function, and the metabolism of sugar and protein.

GOOD SOURCES OF POTASSIUM Yogurt, pulses, soya flour, nuts, seeds, green vegetables, potatoes, beetroot, chillies, garlic, sea vegetables, rhubarb, bananas, dates, dried apricots, prunes.

INDEX

Page numbers in *italic* refer to the illustrations